My Lebanese Cookbook

My
Lebanese
Cookbook

80+ Family Favorites
Made Simple

TARIK FALLOUS

ROCKRIDGE
PRESS

For general information on our other products and services or to obtain technical support, please contact our Customer Care Department within the United States at (866) 744-2665, or outside the United States at (510) 253-0500.

Rockridge Press publishes its books in a variety of electronic and print formats. Some content that appears in print may not be available in electronic books, and vice versa.

Interior and Cover Designer: Julie Schrader
Art Producer: Sara Feinstein
Editor: Pam Kingsley
Production Manager: Jose Olivera
Production Editor: Melissa Edeburn

Photography © 2019 Evi Abeler, cover, p. 8, 16, 36, 48, 78, 84, 96, 128; iStock.com, p. vi; Shutterstock.com, duplex, p. xii, 114.
Food styling by Albane Sharrard.

ISBN: Print 978-1-64152-740-8 | Ebook 978-1-64152-741-5
R0

To my father, who is no longer physically
present in my life, but whose impact I still
feel every day, and to my amazing mother,
who is always supportive and loving. You both
have created a good man.

Contents

Introduction

WHEN I WAS GROWING UP IN LEBANON, my family's home always welcomed relatives and friends with a table full of delicious food. It was an unspoken rule in our house that no one should sit at the table alone. My father taught me that even the simplest meal can be memorable when enjoyed with others. In Lebanon, eating is a social affair. Lebanese people know that food always tastes best when it is shared.

My mother was a great cook and very resourceful, too. Her kitchen was well kept, and her pantry was well stocked. She was always prepared to make the classic Lebanese recipes that were passed down to her by her own relatives.

Our kitchen was always busy. My mother, my aunts, my neighbors—everyone around me was cooking all the time. I developed a discerning palate at a very young age, and I learned how to use each ingredient in my mother's kitchen in my own cooking. I came to understand that a good cook can bring each ingredient's character to life at the table.

When I came to the United States as a 19-year-old student, Lebanese food was not very popular. Sure, I could find "Middle Eastern" or "Mediterranean" cuisine in New York City, where I was studying. But I missed the authentic Lebanese dishes of my homeland.

I discovered that there were a few restaurants in Brooklyn serving Lebanese cuisine. They were an hour and 15 minutes away by train for me, but every Thursday, I would skip out of my evening class early to go. *Tabeekh* (home-cooked meals) such as *Bamiye Bi Lahme* (okra stew with lamb) didn't taste exactly like my mother's, but the resemblance was sufficient. I would order one to eat at the restaurant and several more to take home.

I learned to cook so that I could continue to enjoy the foods from my youth in Lebanon. I developed a passion for using cooking as a way of expressing feelings, sharing memories, and creating new ones. In 2014, this passion led me to open my own Lebanese restaurant, Au Za'atar, in the East Village.

In the years since I first arrived in the United States, Lebanese food has become increasingly popular thanks to its unique flavors, healthiness, and variety. It is rustic, savory, and generally easy to make. I think you will find that the recipes in this book will allow you to make aromatic and zesty food with just a few basic ingredients.

Lebanese cuisine dates back thousands of years and reflects influences from both the East and the West. The Ottomans occupied Lebanon from the 1500s to the early 1900s. They introduced lamb, olive oil, and a variety of dishes such as the yogurt cheese dip *labne* and stuffed vegetables. They also introduced bread, coffee, and *baklawa* to the region. Then, the French defeated the Ottomans in World War I and brought their refined culinary influence.

Even though Lebanese cuisine relies on a relatively small number of core ingredients, you'll find a wide variety of regional Lebanese cooking styles. In the mountains, for instance, the food is meat-oriented; on the coast, fish and seafood are emphasized. But what you'll find all over Lebanon is a style of cooking that relies on fresh, seasonal produce and other healthy, flavorful ingredients.

Mezze, the assortment of small plates that are served together as a meal or as an appetizer course, are a hallmark of Lebanese cuisine. These small plates offer an array of colors, flavors, textures, and aromas. They are shared and passed around the table, creating a convivial environment that encourages conversation.

Mezze can be as simple as raw or pickled vegetables, toasted nuts, hummus, baba ghanoush, and pita bread, which is used to scoop up dips and salads. An elaborate mezze spread might also include grilled marinated seafood, skewered meats, a variety of cooked and raw salads, meat- or vegetable-filled pastries, and an assortment of desserts. A more extensive meal would follow up the mezze with grilled meat (usually lamb), stew (meat or vegetable), grain dishes, vegetable side dishes, and dessert.

The cold weather in Lebanon calls for hearty stews featuring both vegetables and meats (especially lamb), ladled over rice pilaf or rice pilaf with vermicelli. Grilled meats, roasted or baked chicken, and broiled or fried fish serve as centerpieces for meals, but they are always complemented by an assortment of vegetables and grains. Desserts range from light and fruity to rich and sweet.

Through cooking, I have learned to appreciate all the textures and flavors of Lebanese cuisine. As a child, I had no appreciation for okra stew with lamb, Bamiye Bi Lahme. I remember picking the meat out of the pot and passing the okra to my sister. Now Bamiye Bi Lahme is one of my favorite dishes. Making the recipes in this book will give you an opportunity to explore new flavor profiles and perhaps to revisit ingredients that may not be your favorites. Whether you are rediscovering Lebanese food or exploring it for the first time, this book will enable you to bring it to life in your own kitchen.

✳ Healthy and Flavorful ✳

Lebanese food is not only delicious, but also one of the world's healthiest. Lebanese cuisine often features meats, but its focus is vegetables. It also relies heavily on fruits, grains, and fresh seafood. Animal fats are used sparingly.

Farm-to-table dining was a way of life in Lebanon long before it became a trend in the United States. Organic food is what my grandparents considered everyday food. Even now, people in certain Lebanese towns and villages consume only locally grown and hand-picked produce. And everywhere in Lebanon, people grow their own fresh herbs and vegetables, which they use for side dishes, fresh salads, stews, and other dishes, with or without meat, and which they often eat raw or pickled.

You won't find heavy sauces in Lebanese cooking. Instead, the cuisine gets its signature flavors from fresh herbs, spices, quality olive oil, aromatics such as garlic, and citrus juices. Fresh garlic, lemon juice, and extra-virgin olive oil are quintessential ingredients in Lebanese cuisine. They balance the earthy flavors for which the cuisine is known and are combined to make salad dressings and marinades for chicken and meat dishes.

Whole grains, such as bulgur and freekeh, have always been part of the Lebanese table. They are often served as side dishes or used as a base layer for stews.

Seeds and nuts are also used extensively in Lebanese cooking. Sesame seeds, in particular, are common in Middle Eastern foods and are used whole, ground up into tahini paste, or pressed for their oil. Nuts, including walnuts and pistachios, are commonly used to garnish rice dishes or stews or to give body to sauces and dips.

What Is Authentic Lebanese Cuisine?

"Authenticity" is hard to define within Lebanese cuisine because each region, village, family, and cook has its own take on Lebanese cooking. One way that Lebanese cooks put their own stamp on their dishes is through their formulation of the common spice blends za'atar and 7-spice blend. These blends can be influenced by family preferences and by local and regional traditions.

Certain dishes and ingredients are found all over Lebanon, but the person who cooks them always injects them with his or her unique style.

❋ How We Eat ❋

In a Lebanese household, food is a celebration of life that brings everyone to the table. Meals are considered social affairs. When eating outside the home, whether traveling or at parties, Lebanese people consider meals to be social occasions. Making new friends and communicating is always easier to do over a table filled with food. Food also tastes best when it is shared with others.

Traditionally, families in Lebanon were large, so meals were the best opportunity to gather and rejoice around food that would appeal to everyone. The variety of the cuisine almost guarantees that there is something for everyone.

Lebanese people have a reputation for being incredible cooks and hosts, but it is not a rigid cuisine. Cooks distinguish their dishes by using a secret combination of spices they'll never fully reveal.

Lunch, especially during weekends and holidays, is usually served around 2:00 p.m. It is an important meal in Lebanese culture. Lunch is a time when the whole family sits together and everyone catches up with one another. Lunch can be a full feast or as simple as soup.

A traditional Lebanese meal starts with an "unchopped salad." This age-old Lebanese culinary tradition is simply a bowl of vegetables meant as a palate cleanser and usually includes olives, whole tomatoes, cucumbers, onions, fresh mint, radishes, and half a head of iceberg lettuce. A bowl of nuts, usually served at the start of the meal, is also always present on the table.

After the nuts and vegetables come the mezze. Lebanese cuisine is all about hospitality, and mezze are a sign of hospitality. Mezze include some of the most famous elements of Lebanese cuisine, and this course provides an opportunity to enjoy many different flavors and textures. Cold mezze are vegetarian heaven, as they feature lots of fresh vegetables and herbs. Hot mezze, which can include meats and seafood, are similarly varied. Mezze are always served with pita bread to scoop up the dips and salads.

After the hot mezze come the *mashawi* (grilled meats) or other meat, chicken, or fish dishes, served with another round of cold mezze, which can include potatoes, dips, salads, rice, or another grain.

The final courses are fresh fruit followed by dessert and coffee, either at the table or in the living room.

A Lebanese host will always encourage you to eat a little more and won't believe you if you say you don't have room. The food is prepared with so much love, pride, and passion—the host wants to share as much as possible with you.

Chapter One

The Lebanese Pantry
Mouneh

The Lebanese pantry, or *mouneh*, was born out of a tradition of preserving local and seasonal ingredients and making the most of them throughout the year. Most ingredients can be easily found year-round, in Lebanon and the United States.

That said, one of the main reasons people don't cook the food they love is that they can't find the ingredients they need. The following guide is a list of pantry ingredients that will make it possible for you to cook delicious and satisfying Lebanese meals. I recommend stocking your pantry with these simple ingredients.

Many of these ingredients can be found in general supermarkets in the United States. For harder-to-find ingredients, look for a Middle Eastern grocery store or order them online (see page 134 for a list of online outlets). Having these basics on hand will make it simpler and more joyful for you to cook Lebanese food.

There is a very old Lebanese saying that is used to compliment a person's cooking: You say someone has *nafas bil akel*. The literal translation is "you have a good breath in food," but what it really means is that your love can be tasted in the food you cook. Of course, love is the most important ingredient in any type of cooking, and that is true of Lebanese cuisine as well. Love the cuisine, love the dish you are preparing, love the ingredients you are using, and most importantly, love the people you are cooking for. Follow this guide, and your food can't help but be well received.

❄ Herbs, Spices, Spice Mixes, ❄ and Other Aromatics

What follows are the most common flavorings, fresh and dried, used in Lebanese cooking. To preserve the best flavor for dried spices and herbs, store them in an airtight container away from light and heat for up to a year. Whole spices will keep their flavor longer than ground.

CILANTRO *(kezbara)* is a fresh herb used in Lebanese cuisine. To keep cilantro fresh, place it in water in a glass jar, with the stem ends submerged. Cover loosely with a plastic bag, and store in the refrigerator for up to a week.

CINNAMON *(erfeh)* is used both in whole stick form and ground. It is mostly used in meat recipes and other savory dishes, rarely for sweets.

CORIANDER *(kezbara nashfeh)* is the dried seed of the cilantro plant. It can be used ground or whole. I like to use it in combination with cilantro to underscore the flavor.

CUMIN *(kammoon)* is a seed that can be used whole or ground. In some regions of Lebanon, cumin is used in most dishes. In other parts of the country, cumin is not used at all. I like to use it when cooking certain lentils and beans because it is a digestive aid.

GARLIC *(toum)* is used heavily in Lebanese cooking. It is considered to be one of the ingredients that gives Lebanese dishes their characteristic flavor. There is a huge difference between fresh garlic and garlic that has been stored for a long time. Always try to use the freshest garlic you can. If you use garlic often, you'll naturally replenish it regularly, ensuring that what you have is fresh. If you use it rarely, rather than keeping old heads of garlic around, buy fresh ones just before using. One bad garlic clove can ruin an entire dish. Store garlic in a cool dark place, or peel the cloves and store them in an airtight jar in the refrigerator for up to one week.

LEBANESE 7-SPICE SEASONING *(baharat)* is a versatile traditional spice mixture that bursts with flavor. It is added to just about every Lebanese cooked dish, including meat and chicken dishes and vegetable stews. It is a combination of allspice, cumin, cinnamon, ground ginger, coriander, cardamom, and black pepper. As with other seasoning blends, each region and family has its own unique formula for making this spice mixture, varying the proportions according to preference.

LEMON *(lamoon)* is also used frequently. The basic Lebanese dressing and marinade is made from lemon, garlic, and extra-virgin olive oil. A final squeeze of lemon makes such a difference in so many preparations. And if you feel your dish is missing something, add a touch of lemon. When life gives you lemons, keep them, because you will be using a lot of lemons in this book. Store lemons in a bowl on your countertop or in the refrigerator to keep them fresh.

MAHLAB *(mahlab)* is made from the pits of the wild St. Lucie cherry, which are ground into a powder and used to add flavor to baked goods, pastries, and cookies. When it first hits your tongue, it tastes like cherries, almonds, and roses with a hint of vanilla. It has a slightly bitter aftertaste. The flavor has been described as being somewhere between bitter almond and nutmeg. Its flavor deteriorates quickly once ground, so it is best to grind it just before using.

MINT *(na'ana)* is one of the most common fresh herbs in the Lebanese kitchen. It is chopped and sprinkled on salads, yogurt, labne, and eggs; stirred into sauces and many other dishes; or added to a sandwich or *manoushe*. It is also steeped in hot water to make a simple mint tea. Just like other green leafy herbs, it can be stored with the stems submerged in water in a glass jar covered with a plastic bag in the refrigerator, where it will last up to a week. Dried mint is also a common ingredient in Lebanese cooking.

ONIONS *(bassal)* are included in almost every savory Lebanese dish. They are also eaten sliced and raw as a side or caramelized and used as a topping.

PARSLEY *(ba'adounis)* is also an important ingredient for Lebanese cooks, who use what is known in the United States as Italian or flat-leaf parsley. It has a more robust flavor than the curly parsley that is used as a garnish. When you bring fresh parsley home from the market, be sure to wash it very well, as it can sometimes be quite sandy. Once washed and dried, place it with the stem ends submerged in water in a glass jar. Cover loosely with plastic and store in the refrigerator for up to a week.

PEPPER PASTE *(majuen elfilfil)* is available in Middle Eastern grocery stores as either sweet pepper paste, mild pepper paste, or hot pepper paste. Using the mild pepper paste is a safer option for anyone sensitive to heat. You also can make it fresh (see page 123).

SESAME SEEDS *(semsom)* are used to make pastries and desserts, such as sesame cookies and crunchy sesame candy. They are also the main component of tahini paste, which is made from ground hulled sesame seeds.

SUMAC *(sumac)* is a spice made by drying and crushing the fruits of the sumac bush, which grows wild all over the Lebanese mountains. It has a tart, tangy, lemony flavor. Citrus is harder to find in the mountains, so sumac is often used instead to add a sour, lemony taste to dishes. Sumac is an essential ingredient in the bread salad *fattoush* and is used to season stews, *kibbe*, salads, or fried eggs. It is also one of the main components of the seasoning blend za'atar.

ZA'ATAR *(za'atar)* is both an herb, called *za'atar akdar*, and a spice blend that is used as a condiment. The spice blend is cherished above all other condiments in Lebanese cuisine. It's a tangy blend of dried wild thyme or marjoram, sumac, roasted sesame seeds, and, sometimes, a pinch of salt. Every region or family makes their own za'atar blend, and the formulas vary just as widely. It is sprinkled on flatbread (Manoushet Za'atar, page 100), croissants, and other baked goods as well as labne, eggs, and salads. You can also mix it with extra-virgin olive oil and use it as a dip for bread. Za'atar is said to be good for the brain, so when I was a kid, my parents always gave it to me before school, especially on exam days.

❋ Other Pantry Ingredients ❋

What follows are items that you'll always find in my kitchen. Many of them are available in large supermarkets (you may have to look in the ethnic foods section for some of them); otherwise, source them at Middle Eastern food stores or online.

BASMATI RICE *(rezz basmati)* is a fragrant long-grain rice. In Lebanese cuisine, it is commonly used in pilafs and served with stews and other rice dishes. If you cannot find it in a general supermarket or a Middle Eastern grocery store, try an Indian grocery store. Store basmati rice in an airtight container or a tight bag in a dry place. It will keep for up to a year.

BULGUR *(burgul)* is a cereal grain made from cracked dried wheat. It is parboiled, or partially cooked, so that it can be prepared relatively quickly. There are four distinct grind sizes, from fine (#1) to very coarse (#4). Two of the most well-known Lebanese dishes—*tabouli* and kibbe—use fine #1 bulgur. The fine and medium grinds are used for salads and baked goods. The coarse and very coarse varieties are better for pilafs or stuffings. Cooked bulgur is also served as a side dish as an alternative to rice or pasta. It also can be served as a hearty main dish. Bulgur can go rancid quickly, so buy it in small amounts, ideally from a source that you know has a high turnover rate.

EXTRA-VIRGIN OLIVE OIL *(zeit zaytoun asli)* is the most commonly used oil in Lebanon. Its thick, rich, and complex flavor can be fruity or peppery. Lebanese farmers drink a sip of olive oil to make sure it is good before using it. Olive oil is used for cooking and in salad dressings. It is also often drizzled generously on dishes such as hummus, baba ghanoush, labne, vegetables, grains, and salads. It can also be seasoned with za'atar and used as a dip for bread.

It is important to use high-quality oil for cooking and in dressings. You can find extra-virgin olive oil in Middle Eastern grocery stores, at your supermarket, or online. Look for extra-virgin olive oil from Spain or Greece. Store olive oil in a cool, dark place away from the stove. It will last up to six months.

FREEKEH *(farik)* is green durum wheat that is roasted, lending it a distinctive smoky flavor. It's an ancient grain that figures significantly in Levantine and North African cuisines.

GRAPE LEAVES *(warra' einab* or *warra' areesh)* are easily sourced throughout Lebanon because just about every house has a grapevine, which grows on a steel structure to protect the vine from the hot summer sun. Most often, the vine and leaves cover the garden, providing shade. The leaves are picked when they are tender and fresh. If left on the vine too long, they toughen very quickly and become inedible. The grape leaf season is short, so most of the leaves are picked in quantity and preserved for the whole year by being pickled in brine and packed tightly into glass jars.

You can find grape leaves packed in jars in Middle Eastern grocery stores or online. The cooking time for preserved grape leaves varies, depending on the quality. Buy the best quality you can find; doing so will save time, since the leaves will cook faster. High-quality brands such as Orlando may also be more economical, since they will have fewer hard leaves that crack and break when filled.

Grape leaves can be tricky, especially if the leaves are brittle, as they will break easily. See Working with Grape Leaves (page 29) for more information.

LEBANESE COUSCOUS *(moghrabieh)* is a large-grain version of the small semolina-based couscous that is more common in the United States. It is often cooked in broth or stock. Moghrabieh should be parboiled in water for five minutes and then cooked in a flavorful broth. Store dried moghrabieh in an airtight container in a dry place for up to a year. Once cooked, it can be frozen for up to three months.

NUTS *(mkassarat)*, including pine nuts, walnuts, almonds, cashews, and pistachios, are served in both savory and sweet dishes. Toasted nuts are often served to guests as part of a mezze spread or as a snack. For savory dishes, nuts are toasted or sautéed in oil or butter and then sprinkled on meat or fish as a garnish. For desserts, nuts are often soaked in water or made into pastes and used as filling. To keep them from going rancid, store them in an airtight container in the refrigerator or freezer.

To toast nuts, heat a bit of oil in a skillet over medium-high heat. Add the nuts, and cook, shaking the skillet, until they are caramel colored and aromatic, about 5 minutes. Remove the nuts from the skillet immediately, transferring them to a plate to cool.

PHYLLO DOUGH *(rekakat),* also spelled "filo," is a paper-thin pastry. It typically comes in sheets measuring 11 inches by 17 inches. It is used to make savory rolls filled with cheese or meat. It also is used to make desserts such as baklawa, which consists of layers of phyllo dough that are brushed with butter, filled with nuts, and drenched in orange blossom syrup. Other desserts, such as *knefe* or *osmalliyeh,* use shredded phyllo dough.

In Lebanon, phyllo dough is available fresh at specialty shops or frozen from the supermarket. In the United States, your best bet is the freezer section of your supermarket, where it can be found in one-pound packages alongside the frozen puff pastry. The frozen variety is nearly as good as the fresh, so I recommend buying that rather than making phyllo dough from scratch, which is very time consuming. Phyllo dough will keep for up to a year in the freezer.

To thaw frozen phyllo dough, place the package in the refrigerator overnight. Once the package is opened, keep the dough covered with a damp towel to prevent it from drying out.

POMEGRANATE MOLASSES *(debs elreman)* is a thick, dark syrup made from concentrated pomegranate juice. It has a tangy and sweet flavor. You can make it from scratch by boiling down pomegranate juice until it's thick enough to coat the back of a spoon. A touch of pomegranate molasses is normally all you need, since its flavor is intense.

Some Lebanese cooks use pomegranate molasses the same way Americans might use ketchup. It is used in savory dishes such as stews, baba ghanoush, or the red pepper and walnut dip *mhammara.* For a simple salad dressing, dilute pomegranate molasses with a bit of water, and whisk it with extra-virgin olive oil and seasonings. Pomegranate molasses does not need to be refrigerated, but be sure to keep the bottle tightly closed.

PULSES *(hboob ibqwlayt)* are the edible seeds found inside the pods of legumes (legumes are any plant that grows seed pods). Fava beans, lentils, and chickpeas are the most commonly used pulses in Lebanese cuisine and are eaten daily in various forms. Chickpeas are used for hummus and falafel, lentils for soup, and fava beans (*foul*) for *Foul Mdammas*.

Chickpeas are especially common in Lebanese cooking. They are added to salads, stews, rice dishes, and more. I prefer using dried chickpeas over canned because doing so allows me to control the salt and eliminate additives. In some dishes, such as falafel, the texture of the dried chickpeas works better. Dried chickpeas are also a more economical choice. I do, however, always keep a few cans of chickpeas on the shelf for those instances when I need to toss together a meal quickly and don't have time to soak the dried chickpeas in water overnight.

Store dried pulses in an airtight container in a dry place for up to a year. Cooked pulses can be kept frozen for up to three months. Canned pulses will last indefinitely.

ROSE WATER (*maa' elzaher*) and **ORANGE BLOSSOM WATER** (*maa' elward*) have a fragrant and delicate floral flavor. They provide the main flavoring for many Lebanese pastries, desserts, sweet breads, and syrups. Rose water is distilled from the petals of the damask rose. Orange blossom water is distilled from the blossoms of the Seville orange tree. I recommend using rose water for pastries, sweet breads, or ice cream; I use orange blossom water in custards and syrups. These condiments do not need to be refrigerated, but be sure to keep the bottle tightly closed. The amount you use will depend on the brand; the intensity of flavor can vary, so use a little to start and add more to taste. I like to use Cortas brand.

TAHINI PASTE (*tahini*) is a paste made of ground sesame seeds and has a nutty flavor. Tahini oil separates from the seed paste over time, so you need to stir it well each time you use it. It is an essential ingredient in hummus and is also used in baba ghanoush, tahini sauce, and desserts like *halwa*, which is made of tahini paste, sugar, and pistachios. There are two types of tahini. One is dark and made from toasted sesame seeds; the other is blonde colored and made from raw seeds. Once the jar is opened, store tahini in the refrigerator, where it will last indefinitely.

VERMICELLI (*sh'ariyeh*) is a Lebanese pasta. It is prepared by breaking it into pieces, frying it in butter or oil, and then cooking it with rice. This mixture is served with stews. Refrigerate cooked vermicelli in an airtight container for up to two weeks. Dried vermicelli can be stored in a cool, dry place for up to a year.

*Baked Omelet with Parsley
(Ejjeht el-Ba'adounis), page 12*

Chapter Two

Breakfast
Terweea'

"Breakfast" in Arabic is *terweea'*, which comes from the Arabic word for quietness, *rawa'*. Breakfast starts very early in Lebanon, and the bakeries fire up their ovens even earlier to bake the daily *mana'ish*, or flatbread. Breakfast is serious business in Lebanese cuisine. It can range from quickly prepared dishes to more involved endeavors that require advance preparation. Either way, breakfast is an event. A simple breakfast might be a plate of Labne (Yogurt Cheese Dip), cheese slices (*halloumi*, *akawi*, and *balade* are popular Lebanese cheeses), tomato slices, cucumber, radishes, mint leaves, and za'atar, accompanied, of course, by fresh Lebanese bread and hot tea. *Mfarket el-Batata* (Eggs with Potato) is another quick and easy breakfast. *Fatet Hummus* (Savory Chickpea Bread Pudding) is a little more involved, but it is one of my favorite breakfasts.

LABNE
Yogurt Cheese Dip

SERVES 18 TO 20 / PREP TIME: 3 DAYS / COOK TIME: 45 MINUTES

Labne is a tangy cheese made of strained yogurt. Drizzled generously with extra-virgin olive oil and served with pita bread or vegetables for dipping, it is a popular breakfast, snack, or appetizer. It can also serve as a healthier alternative to cream cheese. You can turn your labne into *labne mtawmeh* by adding salt and minced garlic and garnishing it with za'atar, sumac, or dried or chopped fresh mint. Always drizzle olive oil on top to add flavor and to keep it fresh longer.

10 cups whole milk

¾ cup plain yogurt

Salt

Extra-virgin olive oil

1. In a large saucepan, bring the milk to a boil over medium heat. Reduce the heat to low, and cook, stirring every 5 minutes, until bubbles form on top, about 45 minutes. Remove from the heat, and let cool until the milk is at room temperature.

2. Stir the yogurt into the milk, then cover the pan with a lid, and place a clean dish towel on top. Set the pan in a dark place, and leave undisturbed overnight.

3. The following day, give the mixture one stir, cover again, then refrigerate for 2 days.

4. After 2 days, line a sieve with 2 layers of cheesecloth, and set it over a large bowl. Pour the yogurt mixture into the lined sieve, and refrigerate until all of the liquid has drained off, about 3 hours. The yogurt should be firm and start to pull away from the side of the sieve when tilted.

5. Season with salt and olive oil. Serve chilled.

PREP TIP: If you don't have the time or inclination to make your own yogurt, you can make labne using store-bought Greek yogurt. Skip steps 1 through 3 and proceed with the recipe beginning with step 4.

MFARKET EL-BATATA
Eggs with Potato

SERVES 3 / PREP TIME: 15 MINUTES / COOK TIME: 12 MINUTES

This dish is typically served in the Lebanese mountains. It is a quick and easy meal that can be prepared for breakfast, dinner, or any time in between. For a heartier version, you can add ground lamb that has been browned in a skillet.

2 large Idaho potatoes, peeled and diced

2½ teaspoons sea salt, divided

½ cup extra-virgin olive oil

5 large eggs

½ teaspoon freshly ground white pepper

½ teaspoon ground allspice

1. Put the potatoes and 1 teaspoon of salt in a large bowl, cover with water, and let soak for 15 minutes.

2. Drain the potatoes in a colander, then pat dry.

3. In a large skillet, heat the olive oil over medium heat.

4. Add the potatoes, and cook until golden brown, about 8 minutes, then add ½ teaspoon of salt and stir.

5. In a medium bowl, whisk together the eggs, remaining 1 teaspoon of salt, the pepper, and allspice.

6. Pour the mixture over the potatoes. Cook over medium heat until the eggs have set, about 3 minutes. Serve warm.

EJJEHT EL-BA'ADOUNIS
Baked Omelet with Parsley

SERVES 4 / PREP TIME: 5 MINUTES / COOK TIME: 20 MINUTES

Ejjeht is Arabic for omelet. This Lebanese omelet is cooked with fresh parsley and is served flat rather than folded. Dress it up by adding vegetables, such as zucchini, cauliflower, or spinach, and serve it warm or at room temperature with sliced tomatoes or pickled vegetables. It's also delicious stuffed into a pita.

8 large eggs

1 cup chopped fresh parsley

1 onion, chopped

¼ cup all-purpose flour

½ teaspoon salt

½ teaspoon freshly ground white pepper

Pinch ground cinnamon

½ cup extra-virgin olive oil

1. Preheat the oven to 350°F.

2. In a large bowl, whisk together the eggs, parsley, onion, flour, salt, pepper, and cinnamon.

3. Heat the oil in an oven-safe skillet over medium heat for 2 minutes.

4. Pour in the egg mixture, and immediately transfer the skillet to the oven. Bake until the omelet has puffed up and set, about 15 minutes. Remove from the oven. Serve immediately.

FOUL MDAMMAS
Fava Bean Stew

SERVES 4 TO 6 / PREP TIME: 5 MINUTES / COOK TIME: 15 MINUTES

This stew is very easy to prepare, especially if you use canned fava beans with chickpeas, which don't need overnight soaking like dried beans do. I like to make it differently each time—sometimes I add hot peppers, sometimes I use tahini sauce instead of water, and sometimes I sauté the onion and garlic first. Serve it with sliced radishes, tomatoes, cucumbers, onions, diced jalapeño peppers, fresh mint, and a drizzle of extra-virgin olive oil and freshly squeezed lemon juice.

2 (15½-ounce) cans fava beans (foul mdammas) with chickpeas, drained and rinsed

½ cup water

4 garlic cloves, minced

Juice of 1 lemon

½ cup olive oil, plus more for garnish

½ cup diced onion

½ cup diced tomatoes, divided

½ cup finely chopped fresh parsley, divided

1 teaspoon sea salt

1. In a large saucepan, combine the fava beans with the chickpeas and water. Cook over medium-low heat until tender and very soft, about 10 minutes. Remove from the heat.

2. Using an immersion blender, mash about half the beans. Cook over medium-low heat until the mixture becomes thick, about 2 minutes. Remove from the heat.

3. Stir in the garlic, lemon juice, olive oil, onion, ¼ cup of tomatoes, ¼ cup of parsley, and the salt.

4. Serve warm, garnished with the remaining ¼ cup of tomatoes, remaining ¼ cup of parsley, and a generous drizzle of olive oil on top.

LAHME W BEID
Scrambled Eggs with Lamb and Pine Nuts

SERVES 2 / PREP TIME: 5 MINUTES / COOK TIME: 5 MINUTES

This simple dish makes for a filling breakfast or brunch. It's also my favorite late-night breakfast-for-dinner kind of meal. The lamb drippings flavor the eggs, and the pine nuts add a crunch and nuttiness that, in turn, complement the lamb.

1 tablespoon extra-virgin olive oil

8 ounces ground lamb

¼ onion, chopped

1 garlic clove, minced

1 teaspoon Lebanese 7-Spice Blend (Baharat, page 121)

½ teaspoon ground cumin

2 fresh mint sprigs, chopped

½ teaspoon sea salt

¼ teaspoon freshly ground black pepper

1½ tablespoons unsalted butter

4 large eggs, lightly beaten

Toasted pine nuts, for garnish

1. In a large skillet, heat the oil over medium-low heat. Add the lamb, and cook, stirring frequently, until browned, about 2 minutes.

2. Add the onion, garlic, 7-spice blend, and cumin. Reduce the heat to low. Cook, stirring occasionally, until the onion is softened, about 1 minute.

3. Stir in the mint, salt, and pepper. In the same skillet, melt the butter over medium-low heat.

4. Add the eggs, and cook, stirring with a wooden spoon with decreasing speed, until the eggs begin to set, about 2 minutes.

5. Serve immediately, garnished with pine nuts.

FATET HUMMUS
Savory Chickpea Bread Pudding

SERVES 4 / PREP TIME: 15 MINUTES / COOK TIME: 15 MINUTES

The essential elements of this dish are tender chickpeas layered with crispy, golden-brown pita chips and a savory yogurt sauce. You can change it by layering various ingredients between the chips and sauce—try shredded chicken, lamb, beef, braised beef tongue, browned ground meat, or fried diced eggplant.

2 pita bread rounds, cut into 1-inch squares

2 (15½-ounce) cans chickpeas, drained and rinsed

1 cup plain yogurt

½ cup cold water

¼ cup tahini paste, thoroughly stirred

2 garlic cloves, minced

Juice of 1 lemon

1 teaspoon sea salt

1 teaspoon ground cumin

½ teaspoon paprika

½ cup chopped fresh parsley

2 tablespoons unsalted butter

½ cup pine nuts

1. Preheat the oven to 350°F.

2. Spread the pita bread onto a baking sheet in a single layer. Bake until the bread is crisp, about 5 minutes.

3. Meanwhile, bring a medium saucepan of lightly salted water to a boil.

4. Add the chickpeas, and simmer until heated through, 2 to 3 minutes. Strain and reserve the cooking water.

5. In a small bowl, stir together the yogurt, cold water, tahini paste, garlic, lemon juice, and salt.

6. Remove the bread from the oven, and arrange on a serving plate. Moisten with some of the reserved cooking water. Spoon the chickpeas on top in an even layer.

7. Top with the yogurt mixture, and sprinkle with the cumin, paprika, and parsley.

8. In a small skillet, melt the butter over medium-high heat. Add the pine nuts, and cook until beginning to brown, 2 to 3 minutes. Remove from the heat.

9. Spoon the butter and pine nuts on top of the yogurt mixture, and serve immediately.

Hummus (Hummus), page 18

Chapter Three

Mezze
Mezza

Mezze are small plates designed to be eaten in a leisurely manner, stimulating your appetite. You can make a meal of mezze or serve them before a more substantial course of grilled meats, poultry, or fish. Mezze might include vegetables, fish, raw or cooked meats, cheeses, and dips.

A mezze course often begins with *bzoorat* (nuts and seeds), *kabees* (pickles), very young green almonds or fava beans with a dash of salt and extra-virgin olive oil for dipping, and vegetable crudités. Then, a few cold mezze dishes arrive at the table, followed by a couple of hot mezze dishes.

Wine and *arak* (Lebanon's national drink, an anise-flavored liquor similar to ouzo and pastis) are typical accompaniments.

Hummus / Hummus **18**

Mtabal Batengane /
Baba Ghanoush **20**

Mhammara / Red
Pepper and Walnut Dip **22**

Falafel / Falafel **23**

Arnabeet Mekli /
Fried Cauliflower **25**

Mdardara / Rice and Lentils
with Caramelized Onions **26**

Warra' Einab Bil Zeit /
Vegetarian Stuffed
Grape Leaves **27**

Fatayer Sbanek /
Spinach Pies **30**

Kibbe Krass / Fried Kibbe
Stuffed with Spiced Beef
and Pine Nuts **32**

HUMMUS
Hummus

SERVES 4 / PREP TIME: 15 MINUTES, PLUS OVERNIGHT TO SOAK IF USING
DRIED CHICKPEAS / COOK TIME: 30 MINUTES TO 2 HOURS

Hummus is the most popular dish on any Lebanese table. It is traditionally served plain
or topped with meat and pine nuts. It is typically flavored with lemon and garlic
and served with pita bread, as a dip for vegetables, or as a spread for sandwiches.
Canned chickpeas don't need soaking and usually need only about 30 minutes of
cooking, but their flavor differs from that of dried chickpeas, and the texture of
your hummus will not be as creamy.

You can use dried or canned chickpeas to make hummus. Using dried chickpeas
is more economical, but it requires advance planning. Dried chickpeas must be
soaked overnight in plenty of water and then simmered for two or more hours.

1 cup dried chickpeas, soaked in 4 cups cold water overnight and then drained, or 2 (15½-ounce) cans chickpeas, rinsed and drained

8 cups cold water

1 teaspoon baking soda (if using dried chickpeas)

½ cup ice cubes

2 cups tahini paste, thoroughly stirred

¾ cup freshly squeezed lemon juice

1. In a medium saucepan, combine the chickpeas, cold water, and baking soda. Bring to a boil over high heat.

2. Reduce the heat to low, and simmer until tender about 2 hours for dried chickpeas or 30 minutes for canned chickpeas. Reserving the cooking water, strain, and transfer to a blender or food processor.

3. Add the ice, and process until mostly smooth.

4. Add the tahini paste, lemon juice, garlic, and salt. Process to combine. If you want a lighter consistency, add up to ½ cup of reserved cooking water, and process until incorporated.

5. Transfer the hummus to a serving bowl, and drizzle oil on top.

1 teaspoon minced
   garlic

2 tablespoons sea salt

Extra-virgin olive oil,
   for garnish

1 teaspoon paprika

6. Season with the paprika, and serve immediately or store in an airtight container in the refrigerator for up to 3 days.

MAKE-AHEAD TIP: You can cook a large batch of dried chickpeas ahead of time and store them in resealable plastic bags in the freezer for up to 3 months. Let them thaw in the refrigerator overnight or for an hour or two on the countertop before blending.

How to Make Dreamy, Creamy Hummus

Dried chickpeas that have been soaked overnight in water will result in a creamier hummus than canned chickpeas. But whether you're starting with canned or dried chickpeas, you can use three tricks to increase the creaminess of your hummus. First, add 1 teaspoon of baking soda to your cooking water to raise the water's pH, which helps break down the chickpeas. Second, add an ice cube or two to the blender while you are processing the hummus mixture. Third, use a rich tahini paste to help emulsify the mixture.

MTABAL BATENGANE
Baba Ghanoush

SERVES 4 / PREP TIME: 40 MINUTES / COOK TIME: 30 MINUTES

No one really knows where the name of this dish originated. *Baba* means "father," and *ghanoush* means "overindulged," so it follows that baba ghanoush is the "father of indulgent dips." A good baba ghanoush is smoky and tangy. The smokiness comes from broiling or grilling the eggplant until the skin is charred and blistered, at which point most of the skin should be removed. Unlike hummus, baba ghanoush should be chunky. It is usually served alongside fish dishes.

3 medium eggplants

6 garlic cloves, peeled

½ cup freshly squeezed lemon juice

¼ cup tahini paste, thoroughly stirred

2 tablespoons extra-virgin olive oil

2 teaspoons sea salt

Pita bread or vegetable sticks, for dipping

1. Preheat the oven to 450°F.

2. With a sharp knife, make small slits all over the skin of each eggplant. This will allow the steam to be released during cooking, which ensures that the eggplants will cook evenly. Stuff the garlic into the slits.

3. Place the eggplants on a stovetop burner. Using heat-resistant tongs, cook, turning every 2 minutes, making sure the skins blister and blacken all over, about 5 minutes. Transfer to a baking sheet.

4. Transfer the baking sheet to the oven, and bake the eggplants for 10 minutes. Remove the pan from the oven. Turn the eggplants over, return the pan to the oven, and cook the eggplants until the flesh is very soft, about 15 minutes.

5. Meanwhile, fill a large bowl with ice water.

6. Remove the eggplants from the oven, and submerge each one in the ice water to stop them from cooking further and to make the charred skin easy to slip off.

7. Once cooled, remove and discard the skin, then split the eggplants in half with your fingers.

8. Place the pulp in a fine-mesh strainer set over a bowl, and allow it to drain and release as much liquid as possible, about 30 minutes.

9. In a medium bowl, using a spatula, combine the drained eggplant pulp, cloves of garlic that were inserted into the eggplants, the lemon juice, tahini paste, oil, and salt. (You can also use a food processor to blend the ingredients together if you like, but I prefer to mix the ingredients this way to keep the eggplant kind of chunky, rather than mashed or puréed.) Serve immediately with pita bread.

MAKE-AHEAD TIP:
This dish will keep in an airtight container in the refrigerator for up to 2 days; bring to room temperature before serving.

MHAMMARA
Red Pepper and Walnut Dip
SERVES 4 / PREP TIME: 15 MINUTES

Lebanon is not well known for spicy dishes, but when Armenians fled the Ottoman authorities in 1915, many of them came to Lebanon, bringing with them many dishes that incorporate hot chiles. This Armenian-influenced dish has become an essential offering of the Lebanese mezze table. It's earthy and sweet as well as spicy, making it perfect as a dip for pita bread or vegetables or as a sandwich spread—for example, you might also slather it on pita bread and bake it for a couple of minutes before adding a topping of grilled chicken or braised meat.

2 red bell peppers, roasted (see Prep Tip)

1 cup walnut pieces, toasted

½ cup toasted pita bread crumbs

¼ cup extra-virgin olive oil

2 teaspoons pomegranate molasses

1 teaspoon paprika

½ teaspoon ground cumin

½ teaspoon red pepper flakes

1 cup water

¼ cup tahini paste, thoroughly stirred

1. In a food processor, combine the peppers, walnuts, and bread crumbs. Pulse until the mixture is smooth.

2. Add the oil, pomegranate molasses, paprika, cumin, and red pepper flakes. Process to combine. Transfer to a medium bowl.

3. While stirring continuously, slowly add the water. Continue stirring as you gradually add the tahini paste.

PREP TIP: You can use roasted peppers from a jar, or you can roast them yourself. To roast them yourself, preheat the oven to 500°F. Place the whole peppers on a sheet pan, and roast, turning them twice, until the skins are completely wrinkled and charred, about 30 minutes. Remove from the oven. Once cool enough to handle, remove the stem and seeds, and peel.

MAKE-AHEAD TIP: This dish will keep in an airtight container in the refrigerator for up to 3 days.

FALAFEL
Falafel

SERVES 4 / PREP TIME: 30 MINUTES, PLUS OVERNIGHT
TO SOAK THE CHICKPEAS / COOK TIME: 10 MINUTES

There are many variations of falafel, but cooks from every region agree on one thing: Falafel patties should be golden and crispy on the outside and moist on the inside. Using dried chickpeas as a starting point is essential. Canned chickpeas are too soft to achieve the texture you want in your falafel batter. Flavored with fresh cilantro, garlic, cumin, and coriander, these crisp patties are really tasty on their own. They're even better stuffed into pita bread and topped with a tangy tahini sauce, fresh mint, radishes, and pickled turnips.

2 cups dried chickpeas

12 scallions, chopped

4 garlic cloves, peeled

2 cups fresh
   cilantro leaves

2 teaspoons baking
   powder

3 teaspoons sea salt

2 teaspoons coriander
   seeds

2 teaspoons ground
   cumin

Pinch ground nutmeg

Pinch cayenne (optional)

1 tablespoon flour
   (optional)

4 cups vegetable oil

Tahini Sauce (Tahini,
   page 124)

1. Pick over the chickpeas, then put them in a large bowl or pot, cover generously with cold water, and let soak overnight. Drain.

2. In a large bowl, combine the chickpeas, scallions, garlic, cilantro, baking powder, salt, coriander seeds, cumin, nutmeg, and cayenne (if using). Mix well. Working in batches, transfer to a food processor, and process into a coarse purée. Transfer each batch of the processed mixture to a bowl before processing the next batch.

3. Once the entire mixture has been processed, knead it together to make sure it holds its shape, working the flour into the dough if a binder is needed.

4. Using your hands or a small ice cream or cookie scoop, form the mixture into 2-inch balls and then flatten the balls into patties.

5. In a deep pot, using a candy or deep-fry thermometer, heat the oil over medium heat to 350°F. Line a plate with paper towels.

(Continued)

FALAFEL
continued

6. Add the falafel patties, and cook, turning once, until deep golden brown and crisp on the outside, about 7 minutes. Using a slotted spoon, transfer to the paper towel–lined plate to drain. Serve immediately with tahini sauce for drizzling or dipping.

MAKE-AHEAD TIP: You can freeze falafel dough for up to 3 months. Press it flat, and store in a zip-top plastic bag.

ARNABEET MEKLI
Fried Cauliflower

SERVES 4 / PREP TIME: 15 MINUTES / COOK TIME: 15 MINUTES

This dish is versatile. It can be a main course or side dish. It is usually served hot or at room temperature, but it can be served cold as well. Substitute any vegetables you like for the cauliflower.

1 cauliflower head, cut into florets

4 cups vegetable oil

1 cup chopped fresh cilantro

Juice of 1 lemon

4 garlic cloves, minced

2 teaspoons extra-virgin olive oil

2 teaspoons ground coriander

1 teaspoon sea salt

1. Put the cauliflower in a bowl, cover with warm water, and let soak for about 10 minutes. Drain.

2. In a deep pot, using a candy or deep-fry thermometer, heat the vegetable oil over medium heat to 350°F. Line a plate with paper towels.

3. Working in batches, using a slotted spoon, carefully add the cauliflower. Fry, turning gently, until golden brown, about 7 minutes. Using the slotted spoon, transfer to the paper towel–lined plate to drain. Repeat until all of the cauliflower has been fried. Transfer to a bowl.

4. While the cauliflower is still hot, add the cilantro, lemon juice, garlic, olive oil, coriander, and salt. Toss, then serve.

MDARDARA
Rice and Lentils with Caramelized Onions

SERVES 4 / PREP TIME: 10 MINUTES, PLUS 1 HOUR TO SOAK THE RICE /
COOK TIME: 55 MINUTES

For this dish, rice is cooked so that it retains its shape as individual grains, unlike *mjadara*, a dish with similar ingredients that is cooked until the rice grains break down. Pair mdardara with Tomato and Red Onion Salad (Saltet el-Banadoura, page 40).

¾ cup long-grain rice

1¼ cups green lentils, picked over and rinsed

6 tablespoons vegetable oil

3 large onions, halved and sliced

1 teaspoon sea salt

½ cup extra-virgin olive oil

1. Put the rice in a bowl, cover generously with cold water, and let soak for 1 hour. Drain.

2. Put the lentils in a medium saucepan, and cover with water. Bring to a boil over medium-high heat. Reduce the heat to medium-low, and simmer until the lentils are tender, about 20 minutes. Remove from the heat.

3. Line a plate with paper towels. In a large skillet, heat the vegetable oil over medium-low heat. Add the onions, and cook, stirring occasionally, until golden brown, about 20 minutes. Remove half the onions to the paper towel–lined plate to drain. Increase the heat to medium. Continue to cook the remaining onions until they are crispy, about 10 minutes. Keeping them separate from the first batch of onions, transfer to the paper towel–lined plate to drain.

4. Add the first batch of onions, the rice, salt, and olive oil to the lentils. Add water to cover. Cover, and cook, without stirring, over very low heat until the rice is cooked and has absorbed the water, about 20 minutes. Remove from the heat. Serve hot, garnished with the crispy onions.

WARRA' EINAB BIL ZEIT
Vegetarian Stuffed Grape Leaves

SERVES 6 TO 8 / PREP TIME: 45 MINUTES / COOK TIME: 40 MINUTES

In Lebanese cooking, grape leaves are often filled with a mixture of either rice and meat or rice and vegetables. You can use fresh grape leaves or jarred grape leaves packed in brine. The former should be blanched in boiling water before filling, whereas the latter should be rinsed well to eliminate excess salt from the brine (see Working with Grape Leaves, page 29). To prevent their burning, the stuffed leaves are traditionally placed on top of other vegetables in the cooking pot.

¾ cup basmati rice

4 tomatoes, finely diced

1 yellow onion,
    finely diced

1¼ cups extra-virgin
    olive oil, divided,
    plus more for garnish

1 cup finely chopped
    fresh parsley

¼ cup freshly squeezed
    lemon juice, plus
    more for garnish

1 tablespoon
    pomegranate
    molasses

1 teaspoon salt

1 teaspoon dried mint

50 large grape leaves

2 potatoes, sliced

2 tomatoes, sliced

1. Put the rice in a bowl, cover generously with cold water, and let soak for 30 minutes. Drain.

2. In a medium bowl, stir together the rice, tomatoes, onion, ¼ cup of oil, the parsley, lemon juice, pomegranate molasses, salt, and spearmint. Let stand for 15 minutes to let the rice absorb the liquid and flavors from the other ingredients.

3. Cut each grape leaf in half along the vein that runs from the top to the bottom of the leaf. Place 1 grape leaf half, shiny-side down, on a cutting board, and put 1½ teaspoons of filling on top. Fold the sides of the leaf over the filling, then fold over the end nearest to you, and roll firmly towards the other end of the leaf. Repeat with the remaining leaves and filling.

4. Line the bottom of a large saucepan with the potatoes and tomatoes. Arrange the filled grape leaves, seam-side down, in a tightly packed single layer on top.

(Continued)

5. Add water to the saucepan to cover the filled grape leaves by about 2 inches. Place a heat-proof plate on top of them to keep them in place. Bring to a boil over medium-high heat.

6. Once the liquid has boiled for 2 to 3 minutes, add the remaining 1 cup of oil, and cover the pot.

7. Reduce the heat to low, and cook until the water has evaporated and the rice in the filling is tender, about 30 minutes. Remove from the heat.

8. Using tongs, gently lift the filled grape leaves out of the pot, and arrange on a serving platter along with the potatoes and tomatoes. Reserve the cooking liquid to store any leftovers.

9. Squeeze some lemon juice and drizzle some olive oil on top. Serve at room temperature or chilled.

MAKE-AHEAD TIP: You can store the filled grape leaves in the refrigerator for 2 to 3 days before cooking. You can also cook them a day or two ahead and store them in their cooking liquid in the refrigerator for a few days.

Working with Grape Leaves

If you've got your own grapevines, you can pick the leaves when they are young and tender and preserve them for making stuffed grape leaves any time of year. To do so, rinse the leaves well and then cook them in salted boiling water (the water should taste like sea water) for about 30 seconds. Immediately shock them in an ice water bath to stop the cooking.

Stack about six of the leaves on top of one another and then, starting from one side, roll them up into a bundle. Pack the bundles on their ends into pint-size canning jars (it's okay to fold the ends over to make them fit), leaving about ½ inch of space on top. You should be able to fit six bundles (or 36 grape leaves) into a pint-size jar.

Add ¼ cup lemon juice to each jar, and then pour about 1 cup boiling water over the grape leaves. The leaves should be completely submerged; add more boiling water if needed. Cover the jars with tight-fitting lids, and store them in the refrigerator indefinitely.

To use the jarred grape leaves (either homemade or store-bought), remove them from the jar and drain them in a colander. Gently unfold and flatten the leaves and rinse them well with cold water. Drain well. Use a paring knife to remove the stem from each leaf before filling and rolling.

You can also use fresh grape leaves for stuffing; just be sure they are picked when they are still tender. Before filling them, drop them in salted water and blanch them for 2 minutes. Drain and then shock them in an ice water bath to stop the cooking.

FATAYER SBANEK
Spinach Pies

MAKES 12 TO 16 PIES / PREP TIME: 4 HOURS /
COOK TIME: 15 MINUTES

Fatayer are small, filled pastries that are popular in Middle Eastern cuisine. They can be filled with spinach, spinach and cheese, meat, or any combination you like. They make for a great snack or party appetizer or a light lunch.

For the dough

½ cup lukewarm water

½ teaspoon active
    dry yeast

¼ teaspoon sugar

2 cups all-purpose flour

¼ cup extra-virgin
    olive oil

1 teaspoon salt

For the filling

8 ounces spinach
    leaves, chopped

1 small yellow onion,
    finely diced

1 teaspoon
    ground sumac

1 teaspoon sea salt

½ teaspoon freshly
    ground white pepper

½ teaspoon red
    pepper flakes

1. *To make the dough,* in a small bowl, combine the water, yeast, and sugar. Let stand for about 10 minutes.

2. In a large bowl, combine the flour and oil. Mix well. Stir in the yeast mixture and salt.

3. Knead the dough well. The dough needs to be elastic and not stick in your hands or the bowl. Form the dough into a ball, and place in a clean large bowl. Cover with a clean dish towel, and set in a warm spot to rise until it doubles in size, about 3 hours.

4. *To make the filling,* put the spinach and onion in a large colander, and season with the sumac, salt, white pepper, and red pepper flakes.

5. Set the colander over the sink, and use your hands to squeeze as much moisture as you can out of the mixture.

6. Transfer the spinach mixture to a large bowl, and add the lemon juice and 4 tablespoons of olive oil, 1 tablespoon at a time, until the mixture is moistened. You don't want to add so much oil that the mixture becomes liquid.

2 ½ tablespoons
   freshly squeezed
   lemon juice

8 tablespoons
   extra-virgin olive
   oil, divided

All-purpose flour,
   for dusting

7. Preheat the oven to 450°F. Lightly flour a cutting board or clean work surface.

8. Once the dough has doubled in size, turn it out onto the lightly floured board, and roll it out to a ⅛- to ¹⁄₁₆-inch thickness. Use a 4-inch round pastry cutter to cut the dough into circles.

9. Place 1 tablespoon of filling in the middle of each dough circle. Fold the circle in half, like a turnover, and seal the edges by pinching them together (dip your fingers in water to help form the seal). Arrange the filled turnovers on a large baking sheet.

10. Transfer the baking sheet to the oven, and bake until lightly golden, about 12 minutes. Remove from the oven. Immediately brush the turnovers with the remaining 4 tablespoons of oil while they are still hot.

MAKE-AHEAD TIP: You can make these hand pies in large batches and store them, baked, in the freezer for up to 3 months. Pop the frozen pies into the oven at 275°F for 10 minutes to thaw and reheat them.

KIBBE KRASS
Fried Kibbe Stuffed with Spiced Beef and Pine Nuts

SERVES 6 TO 8 / PREP TIME: 45 MINUTES / COOK TIME: 1 HOUR

For this dish, a combination of leg of lamb and beef round is best. Serve the kibbe hot or at room temperature with Yogurt-Cucumber Salad (Laban Bi Keyar, page 41) or Tomato and Red Onion Salad (Saltet el-Banadoura, page 40).

For the dough

1 cup fine (#1) bulgur

1¼ teaspoons sea salt, divided

1 yellow onion, quartered

½ teaspoon ground allspice

½ teaspoon ground cinnamon

½ teaspoon freshly ground black pepper

1½ pounds 90% lean ground meat

1. *To make the dough,* put the bulgur in a bowl, and rinse under cold water for a few seconds. Drain, then add water to cover the bulgur, and let soak for 5 minutes. Drain in a sieve, pressing the remaining water out. Sprinkle ¼ teaspoon of salt on the bulgur to prevent it from getting mushy.

2. In a food processor, pulse the onion until finely chopped. Add the bulgur, remaining 1 teaspoon of salt, the allspice, cinnamon, and pepper.

3. With the processor running, slowly add the meat through the feed tube. Process until the mixture reaches a dough-like consistency. Use a rubber spatula to scrape the bowl. As you are processing, add an ice cube or two. This prevents the dough from becoming dry. The dough should be firm and smooth.

4. *To make the filling,* in a skillet, heat ¼ cup of oil over medium-high heat. Add the pine nuts, and cook, shaking the skillet, until they are caramel colored, about 3 minutes. Transfer to a plate to cool.

For the filling

¼ cup extra-virgin olive oil, plus 2 teaspoons, divided

½ cup pine nuts

1 large onion, chopped

1 pound 80% lean ground beef

1½ teaspoons sea salt

1 teaspoon ground allspice

¼ teaspoon ground cinnamon

¼ teaspoon freshly ground black pepper

For frying the kibbe

4 cups vegetable oil

5. Add the onion to the skillet, and cook, stirring frequently, until softened, about 7 minutes. Add the ground beef and cook, breaking up with a wooden spoon, until browned, about 7 minutes. Season with the salt, allspice, cinnamon, and pepper. Remove from the heat.

6. To form the kibbe balls, put the dough in a bowl, and knead it with your hands until it is very smooth. Use a 1½-inch cookie dough or ice cream scoop to make evenly sized balls. Set the balls next to each other, but not touching, on a piece of foil so they don't stick.

7. Fill a bowl with ice water, and add the remaining 2 teaspoons of oil to the water. Wet your fingers with the ice water. Roll 1 ball between your palms until it is even and smooth. Hold the ball in the palm of one hand, and use the tip of the index finger on the other hand to form a cavity in the ball. Work the ball into a thin shell; you want it to be as thin as possible. Dip your finger in the ice water as soon as the dough begins to get sticky. Place 1 teaspoon of filling into the cavity. Dip your finger in the ice water, and gently pinch the opening with your thumb and index finger to seal it. Repeat with the remaining dough and filling.

8. *To fry the kibbe,* in a deep pot, using a candy or deep-fry thermometer, heat the oil over medium heat to 375°F. Line a plate with paper towels.

(Continued)

KIBBE KRASS
continued

9. Working in batches, add the kibbe balls, and fry until browned, about 3 minutes. Using a slotted spoon, transfer to the paper towel–lined plate to drain. Serve hot or at room temperature.

*Chopped Seasonal Vegetable and
Bread Salad (Fattoush), page 39*

Chapter Four

Salads
Salatat

Seasonal vegetables are abundant in Lebanon, and salads made with them are a big part of Lebanese cuisine. Such salads provide a light counterpart to the more substantial meat dishes. The sharp tang of lemon, aromatic fresh herbs, and a good, fruity extra-virgin olive oil can turn the simplest assortment of vegetables into a revelation for your taste buds.

TABOULI
Chopped Parsley, Tomato, and Bulgur Salad
SERVES 4 / PREP TIME: 30 MINUTES

Some dishes allow for variety in their preparation; others must follow the recipe to the letter. Tabouli falls into the latter category. There are a few keys to making a good, authentic Lebanese tabouli. First, the parsley must be washed very well to remove any sand. Second, the stems must be removed and the leaves thinly chopped. Third, the bulgur must be fine (#1) bulgur. Finally, the salad must be served cold. Tabouli is traditionally eaten by scooping it up with hearts of romaine or cabbage leaves, but you can also eat it with a fork.

¼ cup fine (#1) bulgur

¼ cup cold water

8 cups finely chopped fresh parsley (leaves from about 12 bunches)

2 pounds ripe tomatoes, very finely chopped

½ cup finely chopped scallions

1 cup extra-virgin olive oil

¾ cup freshly squeezed lemon juice

1 teaspoon dried spearmint

1 teaspoon sea salt

1 romaine heart, leaves separated

1. Put the bulgur in a small bowl, and add the water to cover. Let stand until the bulgur has absorbed the water and softened, about 15 minutes.

2. Squeeze out the excess water from the bulgur. Transfer to a large bowl. Add the parsley, tomatoes, and scallions. Toss to mix.

3. Just before serving, add the oil, lemon juice, and mint. Season with salt. Serve immediately with the romaine.

FATTOUSH
Chopped Seasonal Vegetable and Bread Salad

SERVES 4 / PREP TIME: 15 MINUTES / COOK TIME: 5 MINUTES

This wonderfully refreshing salad is a staple of the Lebanese table.

1 pita bread

¼ cup fresh lemon juice

¼ cup olive oil

1 garlic clove, minced

2 teaspoons ground sumac, divided

2 teaspoons dried mint, divided

1 teaspoon pomegranate molasses

1 teaspoon sea salt

1 cup quartered cherry tomatoes

4 radishes, sliced

2 romaine hearts, coarsely chopped

2 Persian cucumbers, quartered and cut ¼ inch thick

2 scallions, cut on a bias into thin strips

3 tablespoons chopped fresh parsley

2 tablespoons coarsely chopped fresh mint

1 tablespoon fresh thyme leaves

1. Preheat the oven to 350°F.

2. Cut the pita into 1-inch squares. Spread on a baking sheet in a single layer. Bake until the bread is crisp, about 5 minutes. Remove from the oven.

3. Meanwhile, in a small bowl, whisk together the lemon juice, oil, garlic, 1 teaspoon of sumac, 1 teaspoon of dried mint, the pomegranate molasses, and salt until thoroughly combined and emulsified.

4. In a salad bowl, toss together the tomatoes, radishes, romaine, cucumbers, scallions, parsley, fresh mint, and thyme. Add the dressing, and toss to coat. Sprinkle the remaining 1 teaspoon of sumac and 1 teaspoon of dried mint on top.

5. Add the pita chips, and toss with the vegetables and dressing so they absorb the flavors. If you prefer the chips crispier, simply add them on top without tossing. Serve immediately.

VARIATION: Add 1 cup fresh purslane leaves.

SALTET EL-BANADOURA
Tomato and Red Onion Salad

SERVES 2 / PREP TIME: 5 MINUTES

There is a saying in Arabic that "simplicity tastes the best." This salad spotlights the freshness of the tomatoes. Because the tomatoes are the stars here, choose the best you can find.

¼ cup freshly squeezed lemon juice

1 garlic clove, minced

½ teaspoon sea salt

3 tomatoes, cut into ¼-inch dice

½ cup coarsely chopped fresh mint

½ small red onion, chopped

¼ cup extra-virgin olive oil

1. In a medium bowl, toss together the lemon juice, garlic, and salt.

2. Add the tomatoes, mint, and onion. Toss gently to mix.

3. Add the oil, and toss to coat. Serve immediately.

LABAN BI KEYAR
Yogurt-Cucumber Salad

SERVES 4 / PREP TIME: 5 MINUTES, PLUS 30 MINUTES TO CHILL

This stand-alone summer salad is often found on the Lebanese table. It is frequently served with lentil and rice dishes. Arabic yogurt has a thicker texture and is more tart than European-style yogurt. If Arabic yogurt is not available, use regular or Greek-style plain yogurt and add ¼ cup lemon juice to the mix. The tang of the lemon juice approximates the flavor of Arabic yogurt.

1½ cups full-fat plain yogurt (ideally Arabic), chilled

1 garlic clove, crushed

¼ teaspoon sea salt

2 Persian cucumbers, trimmed and cut into ½-inch dice

1 teaspoon dried mint

1. In a medium bowl, stir together the yogurt, garlic, and salt.

2. Add the cucumbers, and toss to combine well.

3. Let the salad rest in the refrigerator for 30 minutes. Serve chilled, garnished with the dried mint.

SALTET MALFOUF
Cabbage Salad

SERVES 8 / PREP TIME: 10 MINUTES

This healthy salad makes a wonderful side for grain dishes and grilled or barbecued meats. Serve it at your next summer barbecue.

1 cup extra-virgin
   olive oil

½ cup freshly squeezed
   lemon juice

12 garlic cloves,
   finely chopped

2 teaspoons sea salt

1 head Savoy cabbage,
   thick outer leaves
   discarded

4 scallions, green and
   white parts, thinly
   sliced on a bias

½ cup coarsely
   chopped fresh mint

½ cup coarsely
   chopped
   fresh parsley

6 radishes, trimmed
   and thinly sliced

1. In a small bowl, whisk together the oil, lemon juice, garlic, and salt.

2. With a sharp serrated knife, cut the cabbage in half down the center. Cut out and discard the core. Finely shred the leaves, and put in a large bowl. Toss them with your fingers to separate so the dressing can coat them well.

3. Add the scallions, mint, parsley, radishes, and dressing. Gently toss to mix and coat. Serve immediately.

SALTET BATATA
Potato Salad with Lemon and Mint

SERVES 4 / PREP TIME: 10 MINUTES / COOK TIME: 15 MINUTES

This potato salad is low in fat because it uses no mayonnaise. It's perfect to serve alongside meat dishes or even as a meal on its own. Personalize it by adding your favorite vegetables, such as carrots, peas, or bell peppers, or add a sprinkle of cayenne to give it a little heat.

2 pounds Idaho potatoes, peeled and cut into large chunks

2 teaspoons sea salt, divided

1 red onion, finely diced

½ cup extra-virgin olive oil

¼ cup freshly squeezed lemon juice

2 garlic cloves, finely chopped

¼ cup coarsely chopped fresh mint

1. Put the potatoes in a large pot, cover with cold water, and add 1 teaspoon of salt. Cover, and bring to a boil.

2. Uncover, reduce the heat to medium, and simmer just until the potatoes are tender all the way through, about 12 minutes. You want them to be al dente so they don't turn into mashed potatoes when you mix them with the dressing. Drain.

3. In a large bowl, toss together the onion, oil, lemon juice, garlic, and remaining 1 teaspoon of salt.

4. Once the potatoes are cool enough to handle, cut them into small dice. Toss with the dressing until evenly coated. Set aside to cool even more.

5. Once the potatoes are mostly cooled, sprinkle the mint on top. Serve immediately, or cover and refrigerate to serve chilled the next day.

VARIATION: You can substitute scallions for the red onion or parsley for the mint, or do both.

SALTET TARATOUR
Parsley-Tahini Salad

SERVES 4 / PREP TIME: 5 MINUTES, PLUS 20 MINUTES TO CHILL

This salad is a great accompaniment to falafel and fish dishes such as Fried Fish with Caramelized Onions and Rice (Seyadiye, page 50). It's also good on its own or served with pita bread. Because this salad is best enjoyed slightly chilled, I prepare and refrigerate it while the entrée is cooking.

1½ cups Tahini Sauce
(Tahini, page 124)

1 cup chopped
tomatoes (optional)

½ cup chopped
fresh parsley

1 teaspoon sea salt

1. In a large bowl, combine the tahini sauce, tomatoes (if using), parsley, and salt. Toss to mix well.

2. Refrigerate for about 20 minutes, and serve cold.

SALTET HINBEH
Dandelion Green Salad

SERVES 4 / PREP TIME: 15 MINUTES / COOK TIME: 20 MINUTES

Dandelion greens are full of nutrients, including iron, calcium, and antioxidants. They are delicious with halloumi, a semi-hard brined cheese, made from goat's or sheep's milk, that is originally from Cyprus. Dandelion Green Salad is typically made with lots of caramelized onions and extra-virgin olive oil. The flavor is rich and mellow.

2 tablespoons sea salt, divided

2 pounds dandelion greens, tough ends removed

¾ cup extra-virgin olive oil

4 yellow onions, thinly sliced

4 garlic cloves, thinly sliced

1 teaspoon freshly ground white pepper

¼ cup pine nuts or slivered almonds, toasted

2 lemons, cut into wedges

1. Fill a large bowl with ice water.

2. Fill a large stockpot with water, and add 1 tablespoon of salt. Bring to a boil.

3. Drop the greens into the boiling water, and blanch until the leaves wilt, about 2 minutes. Drain, and immediately plunge them into the ice water to stop the cooking. Drain, then squeeze dry. Transfer to a cutting board, and chop coarsely.

4. In a large skillet, heat the oil over medium heat. Add the onions, and cook, stirring occasionally, until very soft and browned, about 7 minutes. Transfer half of them to a serving plate, and transfer the rest to a bowl and reserve for garnish.

5. Add the dandelion greens to the same skillet, and cook, stirring frequently, for 10 minutes. Stir in the garlic, remaining 1 tablespoon of salt, and the pepper. Remove from the heat.

6. Pile the greens on top of the caramelized onions on the serving plate, and top with the reserved caramelized onions. Sprinkle with the pine nuts, and serve immediately with the lemon wedges on the side.

LOUBIEH BEL ZEIT
Green Bean Salad

SERVES 4 / PREP TIME: 15 MINUTES / COOK TIME: 1 HOUR 15 MINUTES

This salad makes for a perfect light dinner or a hearty side. It tastes even better the next day, after the flavors have had time to meld. Serve it at room temperature with some sliced radishes, olives, and pita bread on the side.

1 cup extra-virgin olive oil

6 yellow onions, chopped

2 pounds green beans, trimmed and snapped in half

12 garlic cloves, peeled

4 medium fresh tomatoes, chopped

1 cup canned diced tomatoes

1 teaspoon sea salt

½ teaspoon freshly ground white pepper

1. In a large saucepan, heat the oil over medium heat. Add the onions, and cook, stirring occasionally, until they turn golden, about 7 minutes.

2. Add the green beans, reduce the heat to low, and cook, stirring every few minutes, until they soften, about 30 minutes.

3. Meanwhile, chop 4 garlic cloves, and leave the rest whole.

4. Add the chopped and whole garlic, fresh tomatoes, canned tomatoes with their juices, salt, and pepper to the pan. Stir to combine. Cover, and simmer gently until the beans are very soft and the liquid has mostly evaporated, about 15 minutes. If the beans are still firm or there is still too much tomato juice, continue to simmer, uncovered, another 10 minutes. Remove from the heat. Set aside to cool. Serve at room temperature.

PREP TIP: Dunk a whole head of garlic in boiling water for 5 seconds to make peeling easier.

FASOULYA BEL ZEIT
Lima Bean Salad

SERVES 4 TO 6 / PREP TIME: 10 MINUTES, PLUS OVERNIGHT TO SOAK THE BEANS / COOK TIME: 1 HOUR 30 MINUTES

This salad is served as a mezze or on its own as a vegetarian main dish. Either way, put it on the table with pita bread. Lima beans are traditionally used, but you can substitute kidney or cannellini beans. You also can cook the beans with meat and tomato broth to turn this dish into a stew and serve it hot over rice.

1 cup dried white lima beans, soaked in water overnight and drained

1 garlic clove, peeled

1 teaspoon sea salt

¼ cup freshly squeezed lemon juice

¼ cup extra-virgin olive oil

½ cup finely chopped fresh parsley

3 scallions, green and white parts, chopped

1. Put the beans in a large saucepan, cover with water, and bring to a boil over medium-high heat.

2. Reduce the heat to low, and simmer until tender but firm, about 1½ hours. Keep an eye on the water level, and add more if needed to keep the beans covered. Reserving ½ cup of cooking liquid, strain the beans.

3. In a medium bowl, mash the garlic and salt together to form a paste. Add the lemon juice, and mix well. Stir in the oil and reserved cooking liquid. Add the drained beans, and toss gently to coat.

4. Serve hot, cold, or at room temperature, garnished with the parsley and scallions.

Fried Fish with Caramelized Onions and Rice (Seyadiye), page 50

Chapter Five

Fish and Shellfish
Asmak w Aklat Bahriye

Lebanese cooking showcases a wide variety of fresh seafood. *Bizri* are a favorite fish. They are small and thin, and the Lebanese people love to deep-fry them and eat them like French fries, topped with a sprinkle of salt and a squeeze of lemon juice. *Sultan Ibrahim*, or threadfin bream, is another favorite Lebanese fish. It is similar to bass and cod.

When the Lebanese fry fish, they will often fry thin pieces of pita bread in the oil that was used to fry the fish and serve them along with the meal. French fries are often served with fried or grilled fish, whereas rice is usually served alongside baked fish. Many fish dishes are accompanied by Parsley-Tahini Salad (*Saltet Taratour*, page 44) and lots of lemon wedges.

Fresh fish should have a mild scent; fillets and steaks should be moist and appear freshly cut. When buying whole fish, the saying goes, "the eyes don't lie"; they should be bulging, shining, and clear—not cloudy.

SEYADIYE
Fried Fish with Caramelized Onions and Rice

SERVES 4 / PREP TIME: 10 MINUTES / COOK TIME: 1 HOUR

The origin for the word *seyadiye* is *seyad*, which means "fisherman" in Arabic. This dish is typically made with the catch of the day. I think cod fillets work best because they have a subtly sweet flavor. The caramelized onions complete the dish and make it sensational. The first step of the recipe is to make a fish stock using fish heads. If you don't have the time or ingredients to make the stock, you can substitute fish or lobster bouillon diluted in water. Just be sparing with the added salt because the bouillon is already salty.

For the stock

½ cup extra-virgin olive oil

2 fish heads, preferably cod, but you can use any fish

½ cup chopped onion

1 teaspoon sea salt

1 teaspoon Lebanese 7-Spice Blend (Baharat, page 121)

12 bay leaves

6 cups water

1. **To make the stock,** in a medium saucepan, heat the oil over medium heat. Add the fish heads and onion. Cook, stirring occasionally, until the heads have browned, about 5 minutes. Add the salt, 7-spice blend, bay leaves, and water. Bring to a boil over high heat. Reduce the heat to low, and cook at a slow simmer, skimming any foam that rises to the surface, for 20 minutes.

2. Strain the stock through a fine-mesh strainer into another pot. Discard the solids.

3. **To make the fish,** in a large skillet, heat 1 tablespoon of butter and 1 tablespoon of oil over medium heat. Add the onions and sugar. Cook, stirring frequently, until the onions are golden brown and begin to caramelize, about 15 minutes. Remove from the heat.

4. Meanwhile, in a medium saucepan, cover the rice completely with stock (add more water if needed). Bring to a boil over high heat.

For the fish

2 tablespoons unsalted
butter, divided

2 tablespoons
extra-virgin olive
oil, divided

2 yellow onions, sliced

2 tablespoons
brown sugar

¾ cup basmati
rice, rinsed

2 pounds skinless cod
loin fillets

1 teaspoon sea salt

1 teaspoon freshly
ground black pepper

2 garlic cloves,
finely chopped

3 tomatoes, seeded
and diced

¼ cup freshly squeezed
lemon juice

2 tablespoons chopped
fresh parsley

5. Reduce the heat to medium-low, and simmer until the stock has been absorbed and the rice is tender, about 10 minutes.

6. Stir the rice into the caramelized onions.

7. In another skillet, heat the remaining 1 tablespoon of oil over medium heat.

8. Season the fish with the salt and pepper. Add to the skillet, and cook until the fish flakes easily with a fork, about 4 minutes per side. Transfer to a plate.

9. In the same skillet, melt the remaining 1 tablespoon of butter over medium heat. Add the garlic, and cook, stirring, for 2 minutes. Add the tomatoes and lemon juice. Cook, stirring a couple times, until the consistency resembles cooked oatmeal, about 3 minutes.

10. Remove from the heat. Pour the tomato mixture over the fish, and serve immediately, garnished with the parsley, with the rice and onions on the side.

SAMAK MESHWI BIL FERIN
Broiled Red Snapper

SERVES 4 / PREP TIME: 15 MINUTES / COOK TIME: 35 MINUTES

Because snapper is delicate and can become overwhelmed by seasonings, this recipe relies on the fundamental ingredients of Lebanese cuisine: oil, garlic, lemon, and salt. I add cumin for additional flavor. Serve this dish with Tahini Sauce (Tahini, page 124) and rice or French fries.

2 whole red snappers, cleaned and rinsed

½ cup extra-virgin olive oil, plus more for preparing the pan and brushing the fish

1½ teaspoons sea salt, divided

2 garlic heads, peeled and crushed

2 teaspoons ground cumin

½ cup freshly squeezed lemon juice

1 lemon, cut into wedges

1. Pat the fish dry with paper towels, and make a series of ½-inch-deep cuts through the flesh. Brush the fish with oil, and season with ½ teaspoon of salt.

2. In a food processor, combine the garlic, cumin, and remaining 1 teaspoon of salt. Process until the garlic is finely chopped.

3. With the processor running, add ½ cup of oil gradually in a thin stream through the feed tube. Once the oil is fully incorporated, add the lemon juice in the same manner.

4. Preheat the oven to 400°F. Line a baking sheet with aluminum foil, and brush the foil with oil.

5. Put the fish on the prepared baking sheet. Fill the cuts and cavity of the fish with the garlic paste and lemon wedges. Fold the foil over the fish, and turn the edges to seal.

6. Bake until the fish flakes easily with a fork, about 35 minutes. Serve immediately.

SAMAK MESHWI
Grilled Sea Bass

SERVES 4 / PREP TIME: 15 MINUTES / COOK TIME: 20 MINUTES

I've always loved the drama of grilling a large whole fish. My personal preference is to use a grill basket rather than laying the fish directly on the grill. That way you get the smoky flavor from grilling without any charred flavor and without the fish sticking to the grates. If you do not have a basket, clean the grill grates well before laying the fish on them.

2 whole sea bass, cleaned and rinsed

¼ cup extra-virgin olive oil, plus more for brushing the fish

1½ teaspoons sea salt, divided

1 green bell pepper, seeded and diced

3 scallions, green and white parts, chopped

1 garlic head, peeled and crushed

½ cup chopped fresh cilantro

1 teaspoon Lebanese 7-Spice Blend (Baharat, page 121)

½ teaspoon ground coriander

¼ teaspoon ground cinnamon

2 lemons, cut into wedges

1. Pat the fish dry with paper towels, and make a series of ½-inch-deep cuts through the flesh. Brush the fish with oil, and season with ½ teaspoon of salt.

2. In a medium skillet, heat ¼ cup of oil over medium heat. Add the bell pepper and scallions. Cook, stirring frequently, until browned and softened, about 8 minutes.

3. Add the garlic, cilantro, remaining 1 teaspoon of salt, the 7-spice blend, coriander, and cinnamon. Cook, stirring, until the garlic is fragrant, about 4 minutes. Remove from the heat. Let cool for a few minutes.

4. Fill the cuts and cavity of the fish with the vegetable mixture, and stuff the cavity of the fish with the wedges of 1 lemon.

5. Preheat a grill on high heat.

6. Place the fish on the grill, and cook, brushing with oil every 2 minutes, until the flesh flakes easily with a fork, about 4 minutes per side. Remove from the heat. Serve immediately with the remaining lemon wedges.

SAMAK TAHINI HARRA
Fish with Spicy Tahini

SERVES 4 / PREP TIME: 5 MINUTES / COOK TIME: 10 MINUTES

There are a few versions of this dish. The fish is seared in a pan, then drizzled with spicy tahini sauce. It's topped with pine nuts warmed in butter.

For the sauce

½ cup extra-virgin olive oil

2 garlic cloves, chopped

1 teaspoon pepper paste (see Ingredient Tip, page 55)

1 cup Tahini Sauce (Tahini, page 124)

½ cup chopped fresh cilantro

½ teaspoon ground coriander

½ teaspoon sea salt

For the fish

4 sea bass fillets

Extra-virgin olive oil, for brushing

1 teaspoon sea salt

1 tablespoon unsalted butter

1. *To make the sauce,* in a medium skillet, heat the oil over medium-high heat.

2. Add the garlic and pepper paste. Cook, stirring, for 1 minute.

3. Add the tahini sauce, cilantro, coriander, and salt. Cook, stirring, until coated with the pepper paste, about 2 minutes. Remove from the heat. Cover the skillet to keep warm.

4. *To make the fish,* using a sharp knife, score the skin in 3 or 4 places.

5. Brush oil onto the skin, and rub the salt into the skin and flesh.

6. In a large, heavy skillet, melt the butter over medium-high heat.

7. Lay the fish, skin-side down, in the skillet. Cook until the skin is crispy, about 3 minutes.

8. Gently turn the fish over, and cook the flesh side until it flakes easily with a fork, about 2 minutes. Remove from the heat.

9. *To make the garnish,* in a small saucepan, melt the butter over low heat.

10. Stir in the pine nuts, and cook until they begin to brown, 2 to 3 minutes.

For the garnish

1½ teaspoons
    unsalted butter

2 tablespoons pine nuts

½ cup chopped
    fresh parsley

1 lemon, cut
    into wedges

11. Transfer the fish to serving plates, drizzle with the sauce, and top with the pine nuts and butter. Sprinkle the parsley on top, and serve with the lemon wedges.

INGREDIENT TIP: You can buy pepper paste online or at a Middle Eastern food store. Or you can make your own (see Roasted Pepper Paste, page 123). For a shortcut substitute, swap it with a combination of half chili powder and half cayenne.

SAMAK MA'AT-TARATOUR
Fish with Lemon and Pine Nut Sauce

SERVES 4 / PREP TIME: 15 MINUTES / COOK TIME: 5 MINUTES

When I come home from a long day of cooking in my restaurant and want a quick meal, I open a can of tuna and enjoy it with the sauce in this recipe. But the sauce is even better on freshly pan-seared sea bass fillets.

For the sauce

1½ cups pine nuts

3 garlic cloves, peeled

1 teaspoon sea salt

1½ cups freshly
   squeezed
   lemon juice

For the fish

4 sea bass fillets

Extra-virgin olive oil,
   for brushing

1 teaspoon sea salt

1 tablespoon
   unsalted butter

1 lemon, cut into
   wedges

Leaves from
   3 fresh parsley
   sprigs, chopped

1. *To make the sauce,* in a food processor, combine the pine nuts, garlic, and salt. Process together until the mixture has a dough-like consistency.

2. With the processor running, gradually add the lemon juice through the feed tube, and process until the mixture has the consistency of yogurt.

3. *To make the fish,* using a sharp knife, score the skin 3 or 4 times.

4. Brush oil onto the skin, and rub the salt into the skin and flesh.

5. In a large, heavy skillet, melt the butter over medium-high heat.

6. Lay the fish, skin-side down, in the skillet. Cook until the skin is crispy, about 3 minutes.

7. Gently turn the fish over, and cook the flesh side until it flakes easily with a fork, about 2 minutes. Remove from the heat.

8. Transfer the fish to serving plates. Pour the sauce on top. Serve immediately with the lemon wedges, sprinkled with the parsley.

SAMAK FILET MEKLI
Oven-Fried Fish Fillets

SERVES 4 / PREP TIME: 10 MINUTES, PLUS 2 HOURS TO MARINATE
THE FISH / COOK TIME: 15 MINUTES

With a serving of fries, this dish is the Lebanese version of fish and chips. The fillets are crispy on the outside and juicy on the inside, and, more importantly, they have very few bones, making them easy for kids as well as adults to eat and enjoy. Serve them with Tahini Sauce (Tahini, page 124).

2 pounds grouper fillets

1 cup extra-virgin
olive oil

⅔ cup white vinegar

1 tablespoon
unsalted butter

1 teaspoon sea salt

1 teaspoon freshly
ground black pepper

1 teaspoon chopped
fresh sage

1 tablespoon finely
chopped fresh
parsley

1 large egg, beaten

1 cup bread crumbs

1 lemon, cut
into wedges

1. Put the fish in a bowl or a glass baking dish, and cover with the oil and vinegar. Let marinate in the refrigerator for 2 hours.

2. Preheat the oven to 400°F. Grease a baking sheet with the butter.

3. Remove the fish from the marinade, and transfer to the prepared baking sheet. Season with the salt, pepper, and sage.

4. In a bowl, whisk the parsley into the beaten egg, and pour over the fish.

5. Sprinkle the bread crumbs on top, covering the fish completely.

6. Oven fry until the fish flakes easily with a fork, about 15 minutes. Serve immediately with the lemon wedges.

SUBSTITUTION TIP: If grouper is not available, you may substitute tilapia.

SAMAK BIZRI-MEKLI
Fried Smelts

SERVES 4 / PREP TIME: 5 MINUTES / COOK TIME: 10 MINUTES

These smelts are a perfect weekend or holiday appetizer. Eat them as you would nuts or popcorn. A glass of the anise-flavored liquor arak (called "the milk of lions" in Lebanon) is the perfect accompaniment. Serve with Parsley-Tahini Salad (Saltet Taratour, page 44) and French fries.

¾ cup all-purpose flour

1 teaspoon sea salt

1 teaspoon freshly
   ground black pepper

½ teaspoon
   garlic powder

1 pound cleaned smelts

2 teaspoons paprika,
   divided

2 cups canola oil

1 lemon, cut
   into wedges

1. In a large bowl, stir together the flour, salt, pepper, and garlic powder.

2. Working in batches, add the fish to the seasoned flour, and toss well to coat. Shake off any excess, and transfer to a plate. Season with 1 teaspoon of paprika.

3. In a deep skillet, using a candy or deep-fry thermometer, heat the oil to 375°F. Line a plate with paper towels.

4. Working in batches, add the fish, and fry until golden brown and crispy, about 3 minutes. Using a slotted spoon, transfer to the paper towel–lined plate to drain. Keep warm.

5. Season the fish with the remaining 1 teaspoon of paprika, then serve immediately with the lemon wedges.

AREYDES
Jumbo Shrimp with Garlic and Cilantro

SERVES 2 / PREP TIME: 10 MINUTES / COOK TIME: 10 MINUTES

This easy-to-make dish goes especially well with Parsley-Tahini Salad (Saltet Taratour, page 44).

4 tablespoons (½ stick) unsalted butter

1 tablespoon extra-virgin olive oil

4 garlic cloves, finely chopped

12 jumbo shrimp, shelled and deveined, tails left on

½ cup chopped fresh cilantro

1 teaspoon ground coriander

1 teaspoon sea salt

1 teaspoon freshly ground black pepper

1. In a medium skillet, melt the butter with the oil over medium-high heat. Add the garlic, and cook, stirring frequently, until starting to color, about 1 minute.

2. Add the shrimp, and cook, turning and stirring frequently, until they turn pink, 5 to 7 minutes.

3. Add the cilantro, coriander, salt, and pepper. Toss to mix. Serve immediately.

Chapter Six

Meat and Poultry
Lahme w Djej

When my parents came to visit me for the first time in my tiny apartment in New York, I took it upon myself to cook them a stuffed lamb (I also ordered a few pizzas just in case things didn't work out). I am proud to say that the results were excellent. My parents were impressed and beyond surprised that a 19-year-old who had never cooked a single thing at home was able to make a meal like that. That experience was a turning point for me and marked the beginning of my road to becoming a professional chef.

Meat and poultry have starring roles in Lebanese cuisine. They are not eaten in large quantities, but they feature in stews, kebabs, and casseroles, where they can shine alongside traditional grain and vegetable dishes.

61

KIBBE BIL-SANIYEH
Baked Kibbe Casserole

SERVES 8 / PREP TIME: 15 MINUTES / COOK TIME: 30 MINUTES

In this recipe, kibbe dough is layered with seasoned ground meat and baked. Serve this dish with Yogurt-Cucumber Salad (Laban Bi Keyar, page 41) or a simple tomato salad.

1 tablespoon
  extra-virgin olive oil

1 batch dough from
  Fried Kibbe Stuffed
  with Spiced Beef
  and Pine Nuts
  (Kibbe Krass,
  page 32), prepared
  through step 3

1 cup ice water

1 batch Seasoned
  Ground Meat with
  Pine Nuts (Hashwet
  Lahme, page 118)

2 tablespoons unsalted
  butter, melted

1. Preheat the oven to 400°F. Coat an 8-inch square baking dish with the oil.

2. Press half the kibbe dough into the baking dish, covering the bottom with a ½-inch-thick layer. Use the ice water to coat your hands as you flatten the layer. You want the surface to be very smooth, and the ice water helps accomplish this.

3. Spread the ground meat over the kibbe dough.

4. Make another layer with the remaining kibbe dough in the same manner as the first layer, but form it on a piece of wax paper, then flip it into the baking dish. Press it gently against the ground meat, sprinkle ice water on top, then smooth it out with your hands.

5. Cut a crosshatch pattern into the top layer, cutting through the filling but not all the way through the bottom layer.

6. Next, cut an X into each diamond shape.

7. Brush each piece with a little of the melted butter, which will keep it moist and give it a nice color when baked.

8. Bake until the top is crusty and golden brown, about 30 minutes. Remove from the oven. There will be some juice around the perimeter; immediately brush it on top of the kibbe casserole while it is still hot.

9. Let cool slightly and then cut out the diamond shaped pieces to serve. Be gentle when serving because the kibbe layers may fall apart. Serve warm.

MAKE-AHEAD TIP:
You can freeze this dish either before or after cooking, and it will keep for several weeks. To serve, you can heat it frozen in a preheated 350°F oven.

KAFTA BIL-SANIYEH
Baked Kafta Casserole

SERVES 6 / PREP TIME: 5 MINUTES / COOK TIME: 25 MINUTES

Kafta meat is rich and flavorful, so I like to keep this casserole simple, topping it with just a layer of sliced potatoes. The dish, however, is easily varied to suit your preferences and the availability of certain ingredients. For instance, you can layer sliced tomatoes, onions, or bell peppers (or a combination of the three) on top of the kafta for a festive presentation. Serve with Rice and Vermicelli Pilaf (Rezz Bil Sh'ariyeh, page 87).

½ batch Seasoned Ground Meat with Parsley (Kafta, page 117)

3 cups water

1 teaspoon sea salt

1 teaspoon freshly ground black pepper

1 teaspoon Lebanese 7-Spice Blend (Baharat, page 121)

2 Idaho potatoes, peeled and cut ½ inch thick

2 large tomatoes, sliced

1. Preheat the oven to 400°F.

2. Put the ground meat in an 8-inch square baking dish, and press it into an even layer covering the bottom.

3. In a small bowl, mix together the water, salt, pepper, and 7-spice blend. Pour over the ground meat.

4. Arrange the potatoes on top, followed by the tomatoes.

5. Cover the baking dish with aluminum foil. Bake for 20 minutes. Remove the foil, and bake until the potatoes have cooked through, about 5 minutes.

KAFTA BI TAHINI
Baked Kafta in Tahini

SERVES 6 / PREP TIME: 5 MINUTES / COOK TIME: 25 MINUTES

In my family, we call this "the forgotten dish" because we all love it but rarely think to make it. Because tahini is a rich ingredient, this dish is an excellent winter main course. Serve it with pita bread, pickles, and hot peppers.

½ batch Seasoned Ground Meat with Parsley (Kafta, page 117)

1 batch Tahini Sauce (Tahini, page 124)

2 Idaho potatoes, peeled and cut ½ inch thick

1 teaspoon sea salt

1 teaspoon freshly ground black pepper

1. Preheat the oven to 400°F.

2. Put the ground meat in an 8-inch square baking dish, and press it into an even layer covering the bottom.

3. Pour the tahini sauce over the ground meat.

4. Arrange the potatoes on top. Season with the salt and pepper.

5. Cover the baking dish with aluminum foil. Bake for 20 minutes. Remove the foil, and bake until the potatoes have cooked through, about 5 minutes.

KOUSA BIL BANADOURA
Stuffed Zucchini in Tomato Stew

SERVES 4 / PREP TIME: 15 MINUTES / COOK TIME: 55 MINUTES

Vegetables can be stuffed with rice, a combination of rice and meat, or with meat alone, as is the case here. For the best results, invest in a zucchini corer, which is available online and in many national stores. Don't throw away the flesh you remove from the zucchini—make a small side dish out of it by sautéing it in extra-virgin olive oil with garlic salt and Lebanese 7-Spice Blend (Baharat, page 121).

For the zucchini

1 batch Seasoned Ground Meat with Pine Nuts (Hashwet Lahme, page 118)

½ cup fresh parsley leaves, chopped

8 to 10 small thin zucchini

½ cup vegetable oil

For the stew

½ cup extra-virgin olive oil

1 tablespoon minced garlic

3 medium fresh tomatoes, peeled and diced

1 (14½-ounce) can diced tomatoes

1. *To make the zucchini*, preheat the oven to 350°F.

2. In a large bowl, mix together the ground meat and parsley until thoroughly combined.

3. Core the zucchini gently. First, trim the stem end, then insert the corer three-quarters of the way down the length of the zucchini, twist, and pull out the core. Insert the corer a few more times to shave down the walls of the zucchini, taking care not to push through the side. Carefully fill the hollowed-out zucchini with the stuffing; do not fill them all the way to the top.

4. Heat the vegetable oil in a large skillet over medium heat. Add the zucchini, and brown on all sides, turning them every minute or two, for 6 minutes. Transfer to a 9-by-13-inch baking dish.

5. *To make the stew*, in a large skillet, heat the olive oil over medium heat. Add the garlic and cook, stirring frequently, until lightly browned, 2 to 3 minutes.

4 cups water

¼ cup tomato paste

1 teaspoon sea salt

1 teaspoon Lebanese 7-Spice Blend (Baharat, page 121)

6. Add the fresh tomatoes and canned tomatoes with their juices. Simmer for about 10 minutes.

7. Add the water, and bring to a boil.

8. Stir in the tomato paste, salt, and 7-spice blend, and simmer until slightly thickened, about 10 minutes. Pour over the zucchini. Cover with aluminum foil.

9. Cover the skillet, and bake until the zucchini are tender, about 25 minutes.

KIBBE LABANIYEH
Kibbe in Mint Yogurt Stew

SERVES 4 / PREP TIME: 5 MINUTES / COOK TIME: 15 MINUTES

This Lebanese stew showcases the simplicity and rich flavors of Lebanese cooking. Its creamy yogurt sauce with sautéed garlic and beautifully seasoned kibbe make every bite a pleasure. There are different ways of preparing this dish. I find this way to be the easiest and least time consuming.

1 batch Yogurt Stew (Laban, page 119)

1 batch Fried Kibbe Stuffed with Spiced Beef and Pine Nuts (Kibbe Krass, page 32)

1 batch Sautéed Mint and Garlic (Aliyyet Na'ana w Toum, page 122)

½ cup pine nuts, toasted

1. In a large saucepan, warm the yogurt stew over medium heat.

2. Add the fried kibbe, and stir gently to coat with the yogurt stew. Reduce the heat to low, and simmer until heated through, about 3 minutes.

3. Add the sautéed mint and garlic, and stir gently to mix without breaking the kibbe. Remove from the heat. Serve hot, garnished with the pine nuts.

VARIATION
Laban Immo / Lamb and Yogurt Stew with Mint and Garlic: Substitute 1 batch of Cooked Lamb Cubes for Stew (Lahmet Kharouf La Tabeekh, page 116) for the Fried Kibbe Stuffed with Spiced Beef and Pine Nuts.

SHISH BARAK
Meat Dumplings in Yogurt Sauce

SERVES 4 / PREP TIME: 1 HOUR / COOK TIME: 25 MINUTES

You'll be tempted to eat these dumplings as soon as they are fried. You'll need self-control if this dish is going to make it to the table!

1 cup all-purpose flour, plus more for dusting

Pinch sea salt

½ cup water

Unsalted butter, for greasing the pan

1 batch Seasoned Ground Meat with Pine Nuts (Hashwet Lahme, page 118)

1 batch Yogurt Stew (Laban, page 119)

1 batch Sautéed Cilantro and Garlic (Aliyyet Kezbara w Toum, page 122)

½ cup pine nuts, toasted

1. Lightly dust a work surface with flour.

2. In a large bowl, combine the flour and salt. Stir in the water until the mixture comes together in a dough. Turn it out onto the prepared work surface, and knead the dough until it forms a smooth, shiny ball. Cover with plastic wrap, and refrigerate for 30 minutes.

3. Preheat the oven to 325°F. Grease a baking sheet with butter.

4. Roll the dough out on the work surface until it is paper thin. Using a cookie cutter, cut it into 2-inch circles.

5. Place ½ teaspoon of ground meat in the center of each circle. Fold the dough over and pinch to seal. Pinch the corners together to form a shape similar to tortellini. Transfer to the prepared baking sheet.

6. Bake until golden and slightly toasted, about 10 minutes.

7. Warm the yogurt stew in a large saucepan over medium heat. Reduce the heat to low. Add the baked dumplings, and simmer so they can absorb the tartness from the yogurt, about 10 minutes.

8. Stir in the sautéed cilantro and garlic. Serve hot, garnished with the pine nuts.

YAKNE BATATA
Potato and Meat Stew

SERVES 4 / PREP TIME: 40 MINUTES / COOK TIME: 1 HOUR 25 MINUTES

Stews are a staple of everyday Lebanese home cooking. They feature a richly flavored sauce and are always served with rice, in this case, a pilaf.

1¼ cups vegetable oil, divided

2 yellow onions, chopped

2 batches Cooked Lamb Cubes for Stew (Lahmet Kharouf La Tabeekh, page 116)

1 teaspoon sea salt, plus dash, divided

1 teaspoon freshly ground white pepper

1 teaspoon Lebanese 7-Spice Blend (Baharat, page 121)

3 cups water

1 pound Idaho potatoes

1. In a large skillet, heat ¼ cup of vegetable oil over medium heat.

2. Add half the onions, and cook, stirring occasionally, until soft, about 7 minutes.

3. Add the lamb, and cook, turning every few minutes, until browned on all sides, about 5 minutes.

4. Stir in the remaining onions, 1 teaspoon of salt, the pepper, and 7-spice blend, add the water, cover, and bring to a boil. Uncover, and skim the froth off the surface.

5. Cover and reduce the heat to low. Simmer until thickened to a stew consistency, about 30 minutes.

6. Meanwhile, peel and dice the potatoes. Put in a bowl, cover with water, and add the remaining dash of salt. After 30 minutes, drain, and pat dry with paper towels; do this thoroughly or the oil will spatter upon contact.

7. In a medium skillet, heat the remaining 1 cup of oil over medium heat. Add the potatoes, and cook, stirring occasionally, until browned, about 10 minutes. Transfer to a paper towel to drain.

1 batch Sautéed
  Cilantro and Garlic
  (Aliyyet Kezbara w
  Toum, page 122)

¼ cup freshly squeezed
  lemon juice

Rice and Vermicelli
  Pilaf (Rezz Bil
  Sh'ariyeh, page 87)

8. Add the potatoes to the stew, and simmer for
   15 minutes.

9. Stir in the sautéed cilantro and garlic, and simmer
   until the flavors combine, about 5 minutes. Stir in
   the lemon juice, and let simmer 1 minute. Serve
   over the pilaf.

LAHME MESHWI
Lamb Kebabs

SERVES 4 / PREP TIME: 30 MINUTES / COOK TIME: 15 MINUTES

When it comes to lamb (or beef) kebabs, take it easy with the spices. Let the flavor of the meat shine. Just a little salt and pepper is all you need.

1 pound boneless leg of lamb, cut into bite-size pieces

½ teaspoon sea salt

¼ teaspoon finely ground black pepper

¼ teaspoon freshly ground white pepper

2 tablespoons olive oil

1. In a large bowl, rub the lamb with the salt, black pepper, white pepper, and oil until evenly coated. Cover the bowl with plastic wrap, and let marinate for 30 minutes at room temperature.

2. When you're ready, build a medium-hot fire in your grill.

3. Thread the lamb pieces onto skewers, and place on the grill. Cook to your desired degree of doneness—I prefer my lamb to still be pink in the center, which takes 4 to 6 minutes per side. Remove from the heat, and serve.

DALA'A MEHSHI
Yogurt-Braised Lamb Ribs

SERVES 4 TO 6 / PREP TIME: 15 MINUTES, PLUS AT LEAST 2 HOURS
TO MARINATE THE LAMB / COOK TIME: 2 HOURS 30 MINUTES

**Traditionally, lamb ribs are stuffed with Spiced Rice with Minced Meat (Rezz w
Lahme, page 88), but to simplify the dish, this recipe calls for the ribs to be cooked
on their own, then served with rice and Tomato and Red Onion Salad (Saltet
el-Banadoura, page 40) on the side.**

1¼ cups extra-virgin
olive oil, divided

1 cup full-fat plain
yogurt

2 teaspoons Lebanese
7-Spice Blend
(Baharat, page 121)

2 teaspoons sea salt

1 teaspoon freshly
ground black pepper

1 teaspoon ground
cinnamon

½ teaspoon ground
cardamom

3 to 4 pounds
lamb breast

6 cups water, or as
needed, divided

1 large onion, sliced

4 garlic cloves, peeled

12 bay leaves

12 cardamom pods

6 cinnamon sticks

1. In a large bowl, whisk together 1 cup of oil, the
yogurt, 7-spice blend, salt, pepper, cinnamon,
and cardamom.

2. Add the lamb, and coat thoroughly with the yogurt
marinade. Cover with plastic wrap, and refrigerate
for at least 2 hours and up to overnight.

3. Preheat the oven to 325°F.

4. Remove the lamb from the marinade, reserving
the marinade.

5. In a large skillet, heat the remaining ¼ cup of
oil over high heat. Add the lamb, and sear for
3 minutes per side. Transfer to a large Dutch oven.

6. Add ¼ cup of water to the skillet. Bring to a boil,
scraping up any browned bits from the bottom.
Pour over the lamb, followed by the reserved marinade. Then, add enough of the remaining water
to cover the meat about halfway.

7. Add the onion, garlic, bay leaves, cardamom
pods, and cinnamon sticks. Bring to a boil.
Remove from the heat, and cover. Transfer to the
oven, and braise until the lamb is tender, 1¾ to
2 hours. Remove from the oven.

8. Transfer the lamb to a serving platter, and cover
with foil.

(Continued)

DALA'A MEHSHI
continued

9. Pour the braising liquid through a fine-mesh strainer into a medium saucepan. Simmer over medium heat until thickened, about 20 minutes. Pour over the lamb, and serve.

BAMIYE BI LAHME
Okra Stew with Lamb

SERVES 4 / PREP TIME: 10 MINUTES / COOK TIME: 35 MINUTES

Okra is one of the most popular vegetables in Lebanon. Choose small okra, fresh or frozen. Serve this stew with a pilaf.

½ cup extra-virgin olive oil, plus 1 tablespoon

2 onions, minced

6 medium tomatoes, peeled and diced

2 (14½-ounce) cans diced tomatoes

½ teaspoon Lebanese 7-Spice Blend (Baharat, page 121)

2 teaspoons sea salt

1 teaspoon freshly ground black pepper

1½ pounds baby okra

1 batch Cooked Lamb Cubes for Stew (Lahmet Kharouf La Tabeekh, page 116)

4 cups water

1 tablespoon tomato paste

1 batch Sautéed Cilantro and Garlic (Aliyyet Kezbara w Toum, page 122)

1. In a large skillet, heat ½ cup of oil over medium heat. Add the onions, fresh tomatoes, and canned tomatoes (drain them first). Cook, stirring occasionally, until the consistency resembles cooked oatmeal, about 10 minutes. Stir in the 7-spice blend, salt, and pepper.

2. Meanwhile, in another skillet, heat 1 tablespoon of oil over medium heat. Add the okra, and cook, stirring occasionally, until softened, about 10 minutes.

3. Transfer the okra to the skillet with the onions and tomatoes. Stir gently, being careful to not break or mush the pods. Cook until the okra is tender, about 15 minutes.

4. Add the lamb, and cook until heated through, about 10 minutes.

5. In a small bowl, stir together the water and tomato paste, then add to the vegetables in the skillet. Stir in the sautéed cilantro and garlic, and serve.

BAZILA BI LAHME
Pea Stew with Lamb

SERVES 4 / PREP TIME: 15 MINUTES / COOK TIME: 45 MINUTES

Serve this easy-to-cook dish with a pilaf.

½ cup vegetable oil

1 pound lamb shoulder, coarsely ground

3 onions, minced

1 teaspoon ground cardamom

2 cups water

4 medium tomatoes, peeled and diced

1½ cups diced carrots

1 tablespoon tomato paste

1 pound young peas

2 teaspoons sea salt

1 teaspoon freshly ground black pepper

1 teaspoon Lebanese 7-Spice Blend (Baharat, page 121)

½ teaspoon cinnamon

1 batch Sautéed Cilantro and Garlic (page 122)

Lemon wedges

1. In a large skillet, heat the oil over low heat. Add the lamb, onions, and cardamom. Cook, stirring and breaking up the lamb with a spatula or wooden spoon, until the lamb is no longer pink, about 10 minutes.

2. Add the water, increase the heat to medium, and bring to a simmer. Cook for 10 minutes.

3. Stir in the tomatoes, carrots, and tomato paste. Reduce the heat to low, and gently simmer until thickened, about 10 minutes.

4. Add the peas, salt, pepper, 7-spice blend, and cinnamon. Simmer until the peas are soft, about 15 minutes.

5. Serve hot, garnished with the sautéed cilantro and garlic and a squeeze of lemon.

SUBSTITUTION TIP: You can substitute 85% lean ground beef or ground chicken for the lamb if you prefer.

FASOLIA BI LAHME
White Bean Stew with Lamb

SERVES 4 / PREP TIME: 5 MINUTES, PLUS OVERNIGHT TO SOAK
THE BEANS / COOK TIME: 1 HOUR 35 MINUTES

Serve this stew with Rice and Vermicelli Pilaf (Rezz Bil Sh'ariyeh, page 87).

1 pound dried
white beans

10 cups water

1 tablespoon white
vinegar

4 tablespoons chopped
fresh cilantro, divided

1 tablespoon olive oil

1 onion, chopped

3 tomatoes, diced

2 (14½-ounce) cans
diced tomatoes

1 tablespoon finely
chopped garlic

2 teaspoons sea salt

½ teaspoon freshly
ground white pepper

½ teaspoon cinnamon

¼ cup tomato paste

1 batch Cooked Lamb
Cubes for Stew
(page 116)

2 batches Sautéed
Cilantro and Garlic
(Aliyyet Kezbara
w Toum, page 122)

1. Put the beans in a large bowl, pour in 2 quarts of water, add the vinegar, and let soak overnight.

2. Drain the beans, put them in a large pot, cover with the remaining 1½ quarts of water, and add 1 tablespoon of cilantro. Bring to a simmer over medium-high heat. Reduce the heat to low, and cook until the beans are tender, about 1 hour.

3. In a large skillet, heat the oil over medium heat. Add the onion, and cook, stirring, until golden brown, about 7 minutes.

4. Stir in the fresh tomatoes, canned tomatoes (drain them first), garlic, salt, pepper, and cinnamon. Cook, stirring occasionally, until the consistency resembles cooked oatmeal, about 10 minutes. Transfer to the pot with the beans.

5. Add the tomato paste. Stir for 2 minutes, then cook, uncovered, over medium heat until thickened, about 15 minutes.

6. Add the lamb, and simmer until heated through, about 10 minutes.

7. Stir in the sautéed cilantro and garlic, and serve.

SHISH TAWOOK
Chicken Kebabs

SERVES 4 / PREP TIME: 15 MINUTES, PLUS 30 MINUTES TO
MARINATE THE CHICKEN / COOK TIME: 10 MINUTES

This popular street food is often prepared as part of a weekend grilling feast. The
yogurt tenderizes the meat and helps it absorb the flavors of the marinade. I love to
stuff shish tawook into a pita sandwich and smother it with the garlic sauce toum.

3 tablespoons yogurt

1 tablespoon yellow
    mustard

½ cup olive oil

½ cup fresh lemon juice

1 tablespoon
    tomato paste

1 teaspoon paprika

½ teaspoon dried thyme

1 teaspoon sea salt

¼ teaspoon freshly
    ground white pepper

¼ teaspoon cayenne

¼ teaspoon Lebanese
    7-Spice Blend
    (Baharat, page 121)

⅛ teaspoon finely
    ground black pepper

3 garlic cloves,
    finely chopped

2 pounds boneless
    chicken breast
    or thighs

¼ batch Garlic Cream
    (Toum, page 126)

1. In a large bowl, mix together the yogurt, mustard, oil, lemon juice, tomato paste, paprika, thyme, salt, white pepper, cayenne, 7-spice blend, black pepper, and garlic.

2. Remove any skin from the chicken and cut it into bite-size pieces. Add the chicken to the yogurt marinade and stir to coat well. Cover with plastic wrap, and refrigerate for 30 minutes.

3. Preheat a grill on medium-high heat.

4. Thread the chicken pieces onto skewers, and place on the grill, turning the skewers once, until cooked through, 6 to 8 minutes. Remove from the heat. Serve immediately with the garlic cream on the side.

MOGHRABIEH W DJEJ
Lebanese Couscous with Chicken

SERVES 6 / PREP TIME: 5 MINUTES / COOK TIME: 1 HOUR 10 MINUTES

Moghrabieh (Lebanese couscous; see page 5) got its name from the North African region of Maghreb, which includes the countries of Morocco, Algeria, and Tunisia. Moghrabieh is similar to couscous, but the grains are a bit larger, and the texture is slightly different. This dish can be prepared with chicken, lamb, or both.

8 cups water

½ cup extra-virgin olive oil, plus 1 tablespoon, divided

3 teaspoons sea salt, divided

1 pound (2 cups) moghrabieh

1 whole chicken

3 cinnamon sticks

1 onion, peeled

1 pound pearl onions, peeled

2 tablespoons ground caraway

1 tablespoon ground cinnamon

1 teaspoon Lebanese 7-Spice Blend (Baharat, page 121)

1. In a large pot, combine the water, 1 tablespoon of oil, and 1 teaspoon of salt. Bring to a boil.

2. Add the moghrabieh. Boil for 5 minutes. Drain in a fine-mesh strainer set over a large heat-proof bowl. Set the moghrabieh aside, and return the cooking water to the pot.

3. Add the chicken, cinnamon sticks, and onion to the pot. Bring to a simmer over medium heat, and skim any foam from the surface as it appears. Simmer until the chicken has cooked through, about 30 minutes. Remove from the heat. Set aside to cool a bit.

4. Strain the broth, reserving the chicken and 2 cups of broth for the sauce. Reserve the remaining broth for another use.

5. In a large skillet, heat the remaining ½ cup of oil over medium-high heat. Add the pearl onions, and cook, stirring occasionally, until browned, about 10 minutes. Transfer to a bowl.

6. Add the moghrabieh to the skillet, and cook, stirring, for 10 minutes.

1 (15½-ounce) can
  chickpeas, rinsed
  and drained

¼ cup cornstarch
  whisked with ½ cup
  water until smooth

7. Add the caraway, cinnamon, 7-spice blend, and remaining 2 teaspoons of salt. Stir to combine.

8. Add 1 cup of reserved broth, and simmer until the grains are tender, about 10 minutes.

9. Add half the chickpeas and half the pearl onions, and simmer until the moghrabieh is soft, for a few minutes.

10. In a medium saucepan, heat the remaining 1 cup of reserved broth over medium-high heat until it steams.

11. Add the cornstarch mixture and the remaining chickpeas and pearl onions. Cook, stirring, until the sauce thickens, about 2 minutes.

12. Cut the chicken into large pieces. Discard the bones and skin. Pile the moghrabieh high on a large serving platter, and arrange the chicken on top. Ladle over the sauce until the moghrabieh is covered, and serve more on the side. Serve immediately.

DJEJ W BATATA BIL-SANIYEH
Baked Garlic Chicken with Potatoes

SERVES 8 / PREP TIME: 30 MINUTES / COOK TIME: 50 MINUTES

This simple dish is perfect for weeknight family dinners. It's healthy and delicious and easy to prepare. Lemon is key to the flavor—that tanginess is what sets this dish apart. I typically use Idaho potatoes for this dish.

2 pounds skin-on, bone-in chicken pieces (can be a combination of drumsticks, thighs, and breasts)

1 tablespoon white vinegar

1 cup extra-virgin olive oil, divided

2 teaspoons sea salt, divided, plus more for seasoning

1 teaspoon Lebanese 7-Spice Blend (Baharat, page 121)

4 potatoes, peeled and cut into ½-inch-thick slices

20 garlic cloves, peeled

½ cup freshly squeezed lemon juice

1. Preheat the oven to 400°F.

2. Put the chicken in a bowl, and add the vinegar. Toss to coat well, and let stand for 2 minutes.

3. Remove the chicken from the vinegar, and rinse in cold water. Pat dry with paper towels.

4. Make several slits in the chicken, and rub it all over with ½ cup of oil, 1 teaspoon of salt, and the 7-spice blend.

5. Put the chicken in a 9-inch square baking dish. Add the potatoes on top, and season with a bit of salt. Thinly slice 8 garlic cloves, and scatter on top. Transfer the baking dish to the oven, and bake until the chicken has cooked through, about 45 minutes.

6. Meanwhile, in a blender, combine the remaining 12 garlic cloves, remaining 1 teaspoon of salt, and remaining ½ cup of oil. Blend until the flavors meld, about 5 minutes.

7. Add the lemon juice, and blend until smooth and emulsified, about 5 minutes.

8. Remove the chicken from the oven. Set the oven to broil. Carefully drain off the excess fat and liquid.

9. Pour the sauce over the chicken and potatoes, covering them well. Return the baking dish to the oven, and broil until the potatoes have lightly browned, about 5 minutes. Serve hot.

FREEKEH BIL DJEJ
Roasted Freekeh and Chicken Pilaf

SERVES 4 / PREP TIME: 5 MINUTES / COOK TIME: 1 HOUR 10 MINUTES

This meat and freekeh (also known as green wheat) pilaf makes for a substantial one-pot meal with rich and complex flavors. It can be made with lamb or, as in this recipe, with chicken. The key is to use the meat broth to cook the freekeh.

8 cups water

2 pounds skin-on, bone-in chicken pieces (can be a combination of drumsticks, thighs, and breasts)

5 cardamom pods

3 cinnamon sticks

3 teaspoons sea salt, divided

1 teaspoon Lebanese 7-Spice Blend (Baharat, page 121)

1 onion, quartered

1 cup freekeh

½ cup extra-virgin olive oil

1 teaspoon ground cinnamon

½ cup assorted roasted or toasted nuts (pine nuts, silvered or sliced almonds, and cashew pieces)

1. In a large pot, combine the water, chicken, cardamom, cinnamon sticks, 1 teaspoon of salt, the 7-spice blend, and onion. Bring to a simmer over medium heat, and skim off and discard any foam as it appears. Simmer until the chicken has cooked through, about 30 minutes. Reserving the broth, strain through a fine-mesh sieve set over a bowl, and transfer the chicken to a large plate.

2. Rinse the freekeh well under running water, and remove any debris.

3. In a large skillet, heat the oil over medium heat. Add the freekeh, and cook, stirring frequently, until browned, about 10 minutes. Add the remaining 2 teaspoons of salt, the ground cinnamon, and 2 cups of reserved broth. You should have twice as much liquid as freekeh. If you don't have enough, add more broth. Cover the skillet, and bring to a simmer.

4. Reduce the heat to low, and simmer, adding more broth as needed, until the freekeh is tender, about 30 minutes. Remove from the heat.

5. Discard the skin, bones, and any gelatinous bits from the chicken. Transfer the freekeh to a large serving platter, and arrange the chicken pieces on top. Sprinkle the nuts on top, and serve.

Eggplant with Tomatoes (Masa'at Batengane), page 92

Chapter Seven

Side and Vegetable Dishes
Atbak Janebiye

Lebanese meals always include multiple side dishes. I recommend preparing sides with the same attention as your main course. You will always find a grain dish, such as *Rezz Bil Sh'ariyeh* (Rice and Vermicelli Pilaf), *Rezz Mfalfal* (Rice Pilaf), or *Burgul w Banadoura* (Bulgur with Tomatoes), served alongside meat dishes or as a base for stews. Multiple vegetable-based sides are usually served together at a meal. *Batata w Kezbara* (Potatoes with Cilantro and Cumin), *Balilia* (Warm Chickpeas with Lemon Dressing), and *Masa'at Batengane* (Eggplant with Tomatoes) might all accompany a meat or fish main course.

REZZ MFALFAL
Rice Pilaf

SERVES 4 / PREP TIME: 5 MINUTES / COOK TIME: 25 MINUTES

Whenever my mother made this dish, I hung around the kitchen until it was ready so that I could get the first serving. It is best while it is still a bit moist and steamy. Remember the cardinal rule: Once the water has evaporated, don't stir the rice while it is cooking.

2 cups basmati or other long-grain rice

½ cup (1 stick) unsalted butter

4 cups water

1 teaspoon salt

1. Rinse the rice in cold water, and drain.

2. In a medium skillet, melt the butter over medium heat. Add the rice, and sauté until lightly toasted, about 5 minutes.

3. Add the water and salt. Cover, and bring to a boil. Cook for 5 minutes.

4. Reduce the heat to low, and simmer until the rice is tender and has absorbed all the liquid, about 15 minutes. Serve hot.

REZZ BIL SH'ARIYEH
Rice and Vermicelli Pilaf

SERVES 4 / PREP TIME: 5 MINUTES / COOK TIME: 25 MINUTES

This pilaf is a staple in Lebanese cooking and is served alongside *yakhani*, or meat (beef or lamb), chicken, or vegetarian stews. Try it as a snack between meals. It's wonderful with a dollop of yogurt on top.

½ cup vegetable oil

⅓ cup vermicelli noodles broken into 1-inch pieces

4½ cups water

2 cups basmati or other long-grain rice

½ cup (1 stick) unsalted butter

2 teaspoons salt

1. In a medium skillet, heat the oil over medium heat. Drop the vermicelli noodles into the skillet, and stir every few seconds until browned, about 3 minutes. Be careful: They burn in a matter of seconds. Remove from the heat.

2. In a medium pot, bring the water to a boil. Add the rice, noodles, butter, and salt. Stir until the butter has melted. Cover, reduce the heat to low, and cook for 20 minutes.

3. Lift the cover. If you see small holes in the surface of the rice, that means it's almost ready. Cover the pot again, and remove from the heat. Let stand so that the rice continues to steam for a few more minutes. Serve hot.

MAKE-AHEAD TIP: You can brown the noodles ahead of time and refrigerate them in a shallow airtight container or resealable plastic bag for 3 to 5 days.

SUBSTITUTION TIP: You can replace the water with chicken broth for added flavor. If you are using broth, you may need to reduce the amount of salt.

REZZ W LAHME
Spiced Rice with Minced Meat

SERVES 8 / PREP TIME: 5 MINUTES / COOK TIME: 35 MINUTES

This aromatic rice with savory meat is traditionally served on special occasions and holidays as a stuffing for a whole chicken or alongside a whole lamb.

¼ cup extra-virgin olive oil

2 yellow onions, finely chopped

12 ounces ground beef top round

4 ounces ground leg of lamb

1 teaspoon sea salt

1 teaspoon freshly ground black pepper

1 teaspoon Lebanese 7-Spice Blend (Baharat, page 121)

½ teaspoon ground cinnamon

¼ teaspoon ground cardamom

4½ cups water

1 beef or chicken bouillon cube

1 tablespoon unsalted butter

2 cups basmati or other long-grain rice

1. In a large skillet, heat the oil over medium heat. Add the onions, and cook, stirring, until browned, about 7 minutes.

2. Stir in the beef, lamb, salt, pepper, 7-spice blend, cinnamon, and cardamom. Cook, breaking up the meat with a wooden spoon and mixing it together with the other ingredients, until the meat is no longer pink, about 5 minutes.

3. Add the water, bouillon cube, and butter. Mix well. Stir in the rice, and bring to a boil. Cook for 5 minutes.

4. Reduce the heat to low, cover, and simmer until the rice is tender, about 15 minutes. Serve hot.

BURGUL W BANADOURA
Bulgur with Tomatoes

SERVES 4 / PREP TIME: 15 MINUTES / COOK TIME: 35 MINUTES

This old-school dish is perfect to make when your pantry is running low because it requires just a few ingredients. Similar in texture to risotto, it should be neither too firm nor too runny. It is meant to be a bit spicy and is generally served in the summer with a side of cooling Yogurt Cheese Dip (Labne, page 10).

2 ½ cups cracked (#3) bulgur

6 medium fresh tomatoes, peeled and cut into chunks

¼ cup extra-virgin olive oil

1 yellow onion, finely chopped

3 garlic cloves, thinly sliced

2 (14½-ounce) cans diced tomatoes, drained

1 tablespoon mild pepper paste (see Ingredient Tip, page 55)

1 tablespoon tomato paste

2 teaspoons sea salt

1 teaspoon ground cumin

1. Rinse the bulgur, and let soak in water for 15 minutes. Drain.

2. In a blender or a food processor, purée the fresh tomatoes.

3. In a large skillet, heat the oil over medium heat. Add the onion and garlic. Cook, stirring occasionally, until softened, about 5 minutes. Stir in the canned tomatoes, fresh tomatoes, pepper paste, and tomato paste. Add the bulgur, salt, and cumin. Bring to a boil.

4. Reduce the heat to low, cover, and cook until the bulgur has absorbed all the water and becomes tender, about 30 minutes. Serve warm.

BATATA W KEZBARA
Potatoes with Cilantro and Cumin

SERVES 4 / PREP TIME: 10 MINUTES / COOK TIME: 45 MINUTES

Potatoes are always a great choice when you have a house full of hungry kids to feed. These are roasted to a golden-brown crisp and drizzled with a zingy sauce. Serve them as a snack or a hearty side dish for meat or chicken.

6 Idaho potatoes, cut into thick wedges

¼ cup extra-virgin olive oil

1 tablespoon sea salt, plus pinch, divided

4 garlic cloves, minced

¼ cup chopped fresh cilantro

½ cup freshly squeezed lemon juice

1 teaspoon ground cumin

1 teaspoon ground coriander

1. Preheat the oven to 450°F.

2. In a large bowl, toss the potatoes with the oil and 1 tablespoon of salt. Arrange in a single layer on a baking sheet. Bake, turning them several times, until golden and tender, about 45 minutes. Transfer to a serving dish.

3. Meanwhile, in a small bowl, combine the garlic, remaining pinch of salt, the cilantro, lemon juice, cumin, and coriander. Mix well.

4. Drizzle the sauce over the potatoes, and serve.

BALILIA
Warm Chickpeas with Lemon Dressing

SERVES 2 / PREP TIME: 5 MINUTES

Lebanese people love chickpeas. This simple dish is often eaten for breakfast or as part of a multi-dish lunch or dinner spread. Rich extra-virgin olive oil, fragrant garlic, fresh parsley, tangy lemon juice, and melt-in-your-mouth chickpeas combine to make this dish a satisfying symphony.

¼ cup freshly squeezed lemon juice

3 garlic cloves, crushed

1 teaspoon sea salt

3 cups hot cooked chickpeas

3 tablespoons extra-virgin olive oil

1 teaspoon ground cumin

½ cup chopped fresh parsley

1. To make the dressing, in a small bowl, whisk together the lemon juice, garlic, and salt.

2. Put the chickpeas in a serving bowl, add the dressing, and mix well.

3. Pour the oil on top, then sprinkle with the cumin and parsley, and serve.

MASA'AT BATENGANE
Eggplant with Tomatoes

SERVES 4 / PREP TIME: 5 MINUTES / COOK TIME: 35 MINUTES

Eggplant is very popular in Lebanon and is one of the most common vegetables in Lebanese cuisine. This garlicky dish features fried slabs of eggplant melted into a sweet tomato sauce. Served with a side of pita bread, which you can use to sop up the sauce, this dish makes for a satisfying lunch.

¼ cup extra-virgin olive oil

2 yellow onions, sliced

8 garlic cloves, thinly sliced

2 eggplants, halved and cut into ½-inch-thick half moons

2 medium fresh tomatoes, peeled and quartered

1 (14½-ounce) can diced tomatoes, drained

½ cup cooked chickpeas, drained

½ cup water

1 tablespoon tomato paste

1 teaspoon sea salt

½ teaspoon ground cumin

1 tablespoon pomegranate molasses

1. In a large skillet, heat the oil over medium heat. Add the onions and garlic. Cook, stirring occasionally, until golden brown, about 7 minutes. Add the eggplants, and cook, stirring, for 5 minutes.

2. Add the fresh tomatoes, canned tomatoes, chickpeas, water, tomato paste, salt, and cumin, and stir to combine. Mix well. Reduce the heat to low, cover, and simmer until the eggplant absorbs some of the liquid and the flavors, about 15 minutes.

3. Stir in the pomegranate molasses, and simmer until all the liquid evaporates, about 5 minutes. Serve warm or chilled.

SHORBET ADAS
Red Lentil Soup

SERVES 4 / PREP TIME: 10 MINUTES / COOK TIME: 45 MINUTES

This simple soup is full of flavor and economical because it uses basic pantry ingredients. It is often served as a starter on fasting holidays like Ramadan. A bowl of *Shorbet Adas* with a generous squeeze of lemon juice and some fried pita chips on top is a perfect way to break the fast.

3 cups red lentils, picked over

5 cups water

¼ cup extra-virgin olive oil

2 yellow onions, finely chopped

1 tablespoon mild pepper paste (see Ingredient Tip, page 55)

1 teaspoon ground cumin

¼ cup freshly squeezed lemon juice

1 teaspoon sea salt

½ cup chopped fresh parsley

1. Rinse the lentils, and put in a large pot. Add the water, and bring to a boil over high heat. Reduce the heat to medium-low, and simmer, adding more water if needed, until fully cooked and falling apart, about 20 minutes. If you like a smoother texture, you can use an immersion blender to purée them in the pot.

2. In a medium skillet, heat the oil over medium-high heat. Add the onions, and sauté until golden brown, about 7 minutes.

3. Stir in the pepper paste and cumin. Cook for 1 minute. Transfer to the pot with the lentils, and cook over low heat until the pepper paste is thoroughly combined, about 15 minutes.

4. Stir in the lemon juice and salt. Serve hot, garnished with the parsley.

MFARKET KOUSA
Zucchini and Chickpea Stew

SERVES 4 / PREP TIME: 5 MINUTES / COOK TIME: 50 MINUTES

If there's one thing Lebanese people try to avoid, it's wasting food. I remember my sister accidentally breaking most of the zucchini when coring them for *kousa mehshi* (stuffed zucchini). Instead of tossing them, my mother diced them for this savory, tomato-based vegetable stew.

¼ cup extra-virgin olive oil

2 yellow onions, finely chopped

8 garlic cloves, thinly sliced

1 tablespoon mild pepper paste (see page 3)

6 medium zucchini, cut into 1-inch dice

1 cup cooked chickpeas

2 medium fresh tomatoes, peeled and finely chopped

1 (14½-ounce) can diced tomatoes, drained

½ teaspoon Lebanese 7-Spice Blend (Baharat, page 121)

1 teaspoon sea salt

½ teaspoon freshly ground white pepper

1. In a large skillet, heat the oil over medium heat. Add the onions, garlic, and tomato paste. Cook, stirring occasionally, until golden, about 10 minutes.

2. Add the zucchini and chickpeas, and cook, stirring occasionally, until softened, about 10 minutes.

3. Reduce the heat to low. Stir in the fresh tomatoes, canned tomatoes, 7-spice blend, salt, and pepper. Cook, stirring, until the flavors develop, about 10 minutes. Serve warm or at room temperature.

Ma'amoul (Ma'amoul), page 102

Chapter Eight

Breads and Desserts
Moaganat w Halawiat

No Lebanese meal is complete without bread. It used to be common to see Lebanese women kneading bread dough in large copper basins. They would carry the dough to the bakery, where it was baked in hot ovens. Each morning, you'd see them carrying their baked bread home on large wooden trays. These days, most Lebanese people buy their bread fresh from local bakeries, but the tradition of homemade bread lives on in recipes like pita.

Desserts are also an integral part of Lebanese meals, especially during holidays and on special occasions. *Aiwmat* (Sweet Fritters) and *Mshabbak* (Colored Sweet Fritters) are popular around Ramadan and Christmas. *Mighli* (Spiced Rice Pudding) is served to celebrate the birth of a baby, and *Snaynieh* (Sweetened Cracked Wheat with Anise) often appears to mark the occasion of a baby getting his or her first tooth. But these sweet treats can be eaten any time of the year.

KEBEZ ARABI
Arabic Pita Bread

SERVES 8 / PREP TIME: 20 MINUTES, PLUS 2 HOURS FOR THE DOUGH
TO RISE / COOK TIME: 10 MINUTES

Most Lebanese families pick up fresh pita bread from the bakery every day. It is used to make sandwiches or to scoop dips, spreads, and stews. Any leftover bread is fried or toasted the next day to top fattoush or fish dishes. When you make pita bread, allow it to cool and then cover the rounds or store them in a resealable bag. They will keep for two or three days at room temperature and for up to three months in the freezer.

2½ cups all-purpose flour, plus more for dusting

1 cup cake flour

1 teaspoon sea salt

1 teaspoon granulated sugar

1 teaspoon active dry yeast

1¼ cups lukewarm water

1 tablespoon extra-virgin olive oil

1. Lightly dust a work surface with flour. In a large bowl, sift together the all-purpose flour, cake flour, and salt. Stir in the sugar.

2. In another large bowl, dissolve the yeast in the water, and let sit in a warm place until the mixture bubbles up, about 5 minutes, then stir in the oil.

3. Add the dry ingredients gradually to the yeast mixture, beating to combine.

4. Once a dough forms, turn the mixture out onto the prepared work surface, and knead until smooth and elastic, about 10 minutes. If you are using a food processor or a stand mixer, run the machine for 1 minute, starting at a low speed and gradually increasing it.

5. Dust a large bowl with flour, and put the dough inside. Cover with a damp kitchen towel, and set aside in a warm place free of drafts to rise until the dough doubles in size, about 2 hours.

6. Punch down the dough. Turn the dough out onto the prepared work surface again, and form into a log.

7. With a sharp knife or a dough cutter, cut the dough into 2 equal pieces and then cut each half into equal quarters to form 8 small balls, each a little smaller than a tennis ball.

8. Preheat the oven to 425°F. Place a baking stone or upside-down baking sheet on the bottom rack of the oven.

9. Using a rolling pin, roll each ball of dough out into a flat circle about 10 inches across. Cover the disks of dough with a damp kitchen towel, and let rest for 10 minutes.

10. Working in batches, place the dough rounds directly on the hot baking stone or sheet, leaving space between them to allow for rising, and bake for 3 to 5 minutes. Make sure they don't burn. The bread is ready when a hollow pocket has formed and the bread has slightly browned on the edge and on the top. Serve hot or warm.

COOKING TIP: To warm up pita bread, using heat-resistant tongs, place the bread directly on the stovetop for about 30 seconds on each side.

MANOUSHET ZA'ATAR
Za'atar Flatbread

MAKES 4 (10-INCH) FLATBREADS OR 10 (4-INCH) FLATBREADS /
PREP TIME: 25 TO 35 MINUTES, PLUS 2 HOURS FOR THE DOUGH
TO RISE / COOK TIME: 12 MINUTES

In Lebanon, mana'ish is a go-to breakfast. As for the za'atar that tops it, every region, town, neighborhood, and household has its own blend. I often took my own za'atar paste to the *forn*, or bakery, so it could be used to make this bread, which I carried home still hot. The bread is delicious all on its own, but you can turn it into a free-form sandwich by wrapping it around sliced tomatoes, sliced cucumbers, olives, fresh mint, or labne.

1 cup lukewarm water, divided, plus more as needed

1 packet active dry yeast

3 cups all-purpose flour, plus more as needed

1 teaspoon sea salt

1 teaspoon granulated sugar

2 tablespoons vegetable oil

2 cups extra-virgin olive oil, plus more for greasing

2 batches (1½ cups) Za'atar (Za'atar, page 120)

1. In a small bowl, combine ½ cup of water with the yeast. Stir to dissolve, and let stand until the mixture bubbles up, about 5 minutes.

2. In a stand mixer, combine the flour, salt, and sugar. Mix on low speed.

3. With the mixer running, gradually pour in the vegetable oil. Add the yeast mixture and remaining ½ cup of water.

4. Increase the speed to medium, and continue to knead the dough until it is smooth, shiny, and pulls away from the side of the bowl, about 10 minutes. If you don't have a stand mixer, knead the dough by hand until it is smooth, shiny, and soft, about 20 minutes. The weather and humidity can affect the dough's consistency. If it feels too moist, add a bit more flour, 1 teaspoon at a time. If it feels too dry, add more water, ½ teaspoon at a time. The dough should be smooth and firm.

5. Grease a large bowl with olive oil, and put the dough inside. Flip the dough over to coat all sides with oil. Cover with a damp kitchen towel, and set aside in a warm place free of drafts to rise for 2 hours.

6. Preheat the oven to 400°F. Line several large baking sheets with parchment paper.

7. In a medium bowl, mix the za'atar and olive oil together until you have a paste.

8. Lightly dust a work surface with flour. Turn the dough out onto the prepared work surface, and using a rolling pin, roll the dough to about ¼-inch thickness.

9. Use a round pastry cutter to cut the dough into 4- or 10-inch circles, and put them on the prepared baking sheets.

10. Cover the dough with the za'atar paste, leaving the edges exposed.

11. Working in batches if necessary, transfer the baking sheets to the bottom rack of the oven, and bake until the bottoms of the flatbreads are slightly golden and the edges are crisp, about 12 minutes. Serve hot.

VARIATION

Manoushet Jebne / Cheese Flatbread: Top the dough with a combination of 2 cups of washed and shredded akawi cheese and 2 cups of shredded mozzarella cheese, and bake as directed.

MA'AMOUL
Ma'amoul

MAKES ABOUT 6 DOZEN COOKIES / PREP TIME: 30 MINUTES, PLUS
30 MINUTES FOR THE DOUGH TO REST / COOK TIME: 15 MINUTES

Ma'amoul are a holiday tradition. For Muslims, ma'amoul are traditionally prepared a few days before Eid, the three-day celebration that ends Ramadan, the month of fasting. For Christians, they are served to celebrate Easter at the end of the Lenten fast. Ma'amoul molds hand-carved from olive wood are used to shape the cookies. Each filling has a specific mold. In this recipe, I've given you three fillings to choose from. The dough is sufficient to make a single batch with one filling.

For the walnut filling

3 cups walnuts

1 cup granulated sugar

2 tablespoons clarified butter (see Prep Tip, page 106)

1 tablespoon rose water

For the pistachio filling

3 cups unsalted shelled pistachios

1 cup granulated sugar

2 tablespoons clarified butter

1 tablespoon rose water

For the date filling

3 cups fresh dates, pitted

¼ cup clarified butter

1. *To make the walnut filling,* in a food processor, combine the walnuts and sugar. Process together until they are the consistency of fine crumbs. Transfer to a medium bowl, and stir in the clarified butter and rose water.

2. *To make the pistachio filling,* in a food processor, combine the pistachios and sugar. Process together until they are the consistency of fine crumbs. Transfer to a medium bowl, and stir in the clarified butter and rose water.

3. *To make the date filling,* in a food processor, combine the dates, clarified butter, rose water, and mahlab. Process together until you have a smooth, soft paste. Transfer to a medium bowl.

4. *To make the cookie dough,* in a large bowl, cream together the clarified butter and sugar until light and fluffy, about 3 minutes.

5. Work the flour into the butter-sugar mixture with your hands until it is well incorporated.

1 tablespoon rose water

1 teaspoon finely
   ground mahlab (see
   page 3)

For the cookie dough

2 cups clarified butter

½ cup granulated sugar

6 cups unbleached
   all-purpose flour

1 cup lukewarm milk

½ cup confec-
   tioners' sugar

6. Gradually add the milk, kneading it into a
   soft dough. Let rest at room temperature for
   30 minutes.

7. Preheat the oven to 350°F.

8. Place a walnut-size chunk of dough in the palm
   of your hand. Using your forefinger, press and
   expand the hole in the center of the dough, rotat-
   ing and pressing the dough against the palm of
   your hand until the shell is ¼ inch thick and about
   3 inches long.

9. Place 1 teaspoon of one of the fillings into the
   shell. Carefully close the dough around the filling, forming a sphere. Press the filled sphere into
   a ma'amoul mold. Tap the ma'amoul mold on a
   work surface to release the cookie, then place it
   on an ungreased baking sheet. Repeat filling and
   shaping with the remaining dough and filling.

10. Bake until the bottoms are light brown, about
    15 minutes. Remove from the oven.

11. While the cookies are still warm, dust them with
    the confectioners' sugar. Let the cookies cool to
    room temperature on the baking sheet before
    removing. Store in an airtight container at room
    temperature for up to 4 weeks.

BAKLAWA
Baklava

SERVES 20 TO 24 / PREP TIME: 20 MINUTES / COOK TIME: 55 MINUTES

Baklawa is the general name for layers of phyllo dough and nuts doused with orange blossom syrup (*a'ater*). It can be prepared in a variety of shapes and with different nuts. The key to success is to use high-quality clarified butter and to add the a'ater while the baklawa is still hot, so that it is thoroughly absorbed.

1 cup clarified butter
(see Prep Tip,
page 106), melted,
divided, plus more
for brushing

3 cups chopped
raw nuts

½ cup granulated sugar

1 tablespoon rose water

1 box phyllo dough
(28 sheets), thawed

1½ batches (3 cups)
cold Orange Blossom
Syrup (A'ater,
page 127)

1. Preheat the oven to 300°F. Brush a 10-by-14-inch baking sheet with clarified butter.

2. In a food processor, combine the nuts, sugar, and rose water until the mixture is the consistency of sand. Transfer to a large bowl. Add ¼ cup of clarified butter, and mix to moisten the nuts and sugar.

3. Stack 2 phyllo sheets on a work surface, and brush lightly with clarified butter.

4. Place 3 to 5 tablespoons of the nut mixture along the long edge of the phyllo. Roll the phyllo up around the filling, into a cylinder. Place the cylinder on the prepared baking sheet. Repeat with the remaining phyllo dough and filling, placing the rolls close together on the baking sheet.

5. Brush the tops of the cylinders with the remaining ¾ cup of clarified butter, and cut diagonally into 2- to 3-inch-long pieces. Bake on the center rack of the oven until golden brown, about 45 minutes.

6. Immediately ladle the syrup over each piece to saturate it. Let cool to room temperature before serving. Store in an airtight container at room temperature for up to 1 week.

KNEFE
Lebanese Cheesecake

SERVES 12 / PREP TIME: 15 MINUTES / COOK TIME: 1 HOUR

Knefe refers to both shredded phyllo dough and to this Lebanese-style cheesecake. This is my favorite dessert. On school breaks when I was a kid, I would often stay with my grandparents. Whenever their neighborhood knefe street vendor learned I was in town, he would come very early every morning and stand beneath my window calling my name until I came down to get my daily knefe. You stuff the knefe into a pocket of dough called *kaake* and then smother it with orange blossom syrup. Every region has its own knefe preparation and uses specific cheeses. This version is my favorite.

8 ounces Greek shredded phyllo dough (*kataifi*)

10 tablespoons warm clarified butter, divided (see Prep Tip, page 106)

3 cups heavy cream

¾ cup fine semolina

1 tablespoon granulated sugar

1 cup shredded mozzarella cheese

½ batch (1 cup) cold Orange Blossom Syrup (A'ater, page 127)

¼ cup finely chopped pistachios

1. Thaw the shredded phyllo dough at room temperature for 1 hour.

2. Preheat the oven to 375°F. Coat a 9-by-13-inch baking dish with 2 tablespoons of clarified butter.

3. Put the phyllo dough in a food processor. Pulse until you have a fine texture. Transfer to a large bowl.

4. Add the remaining 8 tablespoons of clarified butter, and toss to mix. Pour into the prepared baking dish, and press down to cover the bottom in an even layer.

5. In a large saucepan, combine the cream, semolina, and sugar. Cook over high heat, whisking, until the semolina dissolves in the cream, the texture begins to thicken, and the mixture bubbles, about 15 minutes. Remove from the heat. Set aside for a few minutes to cool.

6. Sprinkle the mozzarella over the phyllo dough in the baking dish, then pour the cream mixture on top, spreading it to the edges.

(Continued)

7. Bake on the center rack until the crust is golden brown, about 40 minutes. Remove from the oven. Let sit for 5 minutes, then flip the baking dish over onto a serving platter.

8. Pour the orange blossom syrup on top. Let set for a few minutes, then sprinkle with the pistachios, and cut into squares. Serve hot with extra syrup on the side.

PREP TIP: To clarify butter, in a saucepan over low heat, melt unsalted butter; do not let it boil. Using a ladle or slotted spoon, skim off the foamy milk solids that rise to the surface. Ladle the clear butter fat into a container, leaving behind the white milky water (the whey). One pound of butter will yield about 12 ounces of clarified butter. It will keep in the refrigerator or freezer for 8 to 12 weeks.

AIWMAT
Sweet Fritters

SERVES 8 / PREP TIME: 15 MINUTES, PLUS AT LEAST 2 HOURS FOR THE DOUGH
TO RISE / COOK TIME: 1 HOUR

Aiwmat in Arabic means "float." These little round balls of fried dough, crispy on the outside, soft on the inside, and soaked in orange blossom syrup, are easy to make and so much fun to eat. Take it from me, once you start eating them, you'll have a hard time stopping.

1 packet active
   dry yeast

1 teaspoon
   all-purpose flour

1 teaspoon
   granulated sugar

2 tablespoons
   lukewarm water

4 cups pastry flour

¼ teaspoon sea salt

3 cups cold water

6 cups vegetable oil

1 batch (2 cups) Orange
   Blossom Syrup
   (A'ater, page 127)

1. In a large bowl, combine the yeast, all-purpose flour, and sugar. Add the lukewarm water, and stir together with a fork. Set aside until the mixture doubles in size and bubbles appear on the surface, about 5 minutes.

2. In a large bowl, sift together the pastry flour and salt. Create a well in the center of the flour, and pour in the cold water and yeast mixture. Mix together very well, then whisk until you have a smooth, soft, moist consistency.

3. Cover the bowl with plastic wrap, and place a clean kitchen towel over it. Set aside at room temperature to rise until the dough has doubled in volume, at least 2 hours and up to overnight.

4. Remove the plastic wrap, and punch down the dough.

5. In a large heavy-bottomed pot, using a candy or deep-fry thermometer, heat the oil over medium-high heat to 300°F. Line a baking sheet with paper towels.

6. Working in batches of 8 or 10 at a time, using a spoon or an ice cream scoop, drop tablespoon-size

(Continued)

AIWMAT
continued

balls of the dough into the hot oil, keeping space between them so they don't stick to each other. Once the dough floats to the surface, about 5 minutes, flip over gently and continue to cook until golden brown, another 2 to 3 minutes. Using a slotted spoon, transfer to the paper towel–lined baking sheet.

7. While the fritters are still warm, toss with the orange blossom syrup to coat completely. Remove from the syrup, and transfer to a serving plate. Serve warm.

108   MY LEBANESE COOKBOOK

MSHABBAK
Colored Sweet Fritters

SERVES 8 / PREP TIME: 15 MINUTES / COOK TIME: 5 MINUTES

Mshabbak are a variation of Aiwmat. Both are fried and crispy, but the shape and color are different. Whereas Aiwmat are golden brown and shaped like donut holes, Mshabbak are more colorful and cooked into a variety of shapes. The word mshabbak literally means "complicated to separate," and the dough for these fritters is piped into the hot oil in intricate interconnected patterns. Mshabbak are a holiday dessert often served during the holy month of Ramadan or on All Saints' Day. The colors of these fritters are very festive.

1 batch Sweet Fritters (Aiwmat, page 107), prepared through step 3

Gel food colorings, for decoration

6 cups vegetable oil

1 batch (2 cups) Orange Blossom Syrup (A'ater, page 127)

1. Divide the dough by the number of different food colorings you will use. Mix each portion with its food coloring; start with a drop or two of coloring and then add more to get the intensity of color you want.

2. In a large heavy-bottomed pot, heat the oil over medium-high heat to 350°F. Line a baking sheet with paper towels.

3. Put the dough in a pastry bag fitted with a ¼-inch tip. Slowly squeeze the dough in a thin stream in a spiral pattern into the hot oil to form lacy rosettes about 4 inches in diameter (make the outside circle first and then fill in the center with an intertwined design). Cook until golden brown, 2 to 3 minutes. Using a slotted spoon, transfer the fritters to the paper towel–lined baking sheet.

4. While the fritters are still warm, coat the fritters completely with the orange blossom syrup. Remove from the syrup, and transfer to a serving plate. Serve warm.

ASHTA
Cream

SERVES 8 / PREP TIME: 10 MINUTES, PLUS SEVERAL HOURS
TO CHILL / COOK TIME: 10 MINUTES

Ashta is the Middle Eastern version of whipped cream. It is a thick, slightly sweet cream that is eaten by itself; topped with honey, sliced bananas, and ground pistachios; or used as a pastry filling. It can also be used as a topping for fruit salad. It is traditionally made by skimming off the thin skin that forms on the surface of boiling milk, which is a long process that requires a lot of patience. This recipe is quick and easy to make at home but delivers the same rich flavor.

4 slices American-style
   white bread, crusts
   removed

1 cup whole milk

1 cup heavy cream

2 tablespoons
   granulated
   sugar (optional)

1 tablespoon cornstarch
   whisked with ¼ cup
   water until smooth

2 teaspoons orange
   blossom water

1 teaspoon rose water

¼ cup ground
   pistachios

1. Cut the bread into squares.

2. In a medium saucepan, combine the milk, cream, bread, and sugar (if using). Cook over medium heat, stirring occasionally, until the mixture starts to steam, about 7 minutes.

3. Add the cornstarch mixture, and cook, stirring, until thickened, about 2 minutes.

4. Stir in the orange blossom water and rose water. Remove from the heat. Let cool, then transfer to an airtight container, and refrigerate for several hours to chill. Serve cold, topped with the ground pistachios.

VARIATION

Mhalabieh / Simple Milk Pudding: Omit the bread and sugar, and stir in ½ teaspoon of ground mastic along with the rose water and orange blossom water. The mastic (which you can buy online) gives the cream just a hint of pine flavor.

AYSH EL SARAYA
Lebanese Bread Pudding

SERVES 8 / PREP TIME: 15 MINUTES, PLUS SEVERAL HOURS
TO CHILL / COOK TIME: 15 MINUTES

The literal meaning of *aysh el saraya* is "the bread of the mansion." This sweet bread pudding makes for a fancy breakfast or a comforting dessert. Whenever I have left-over cooked French toast, I use it to make the pudding even more decadent.

8 slices American-style white bread, crusts removed

1½ cups packed dark brown sugar

¾ cup water

1 tablespoon freshly squeezed lemon juice

1 teaspoon orange blossom water

1 batch (2 cups) Orange Blossom Syrup (A'ater, page 127)

1 batch Cream (Ashta, page 110)

½ cup ground pistachios

1. Put the bread in a 9-by-13-inch baking dish.

2. In a medium saucepan, combine the brown sugar and water. Bring to a boil over medium heat, stirring until the sugar is dissolved. Continue to cook, stirring, until the mixture turns light brown. Stir in the lemon juice and orange blossom water, and stir for 1 minute. Add the orange blossom syrup, and stir until dark brown. Remove from the heat, and let cool.

3. Pour the cooled syrup over the bread, covering it completely. Cover the dish with plastic wrap, and refrigerate for several hours.

4. Spread the cream on top, and sprinkle with the ground pistachios. Serve cold.

MIGHLI
Spiced Rice Pudding

SERVES 8 / PREP TIME: 5 MINUTES, PLUS 1 HOUR
TO CHILL / COOK TIME: 30 MINUTES

Mighli **is traditionally served by new parents and other family members to guests to celebrate the birth of a baby.**

1 cup rice flour

1 cup granulated sugar

1 tablespoon
ground caraway

1 tablespoon anise
seeds

1 tablespoon ground
cinnamon

½ teaspoon ground
ginger

7 cups cold water

8 teaspoons
unsweetened
shredded coconut

¼ cup chopped mixed
nuts (a combination
of pine nuts,
blanched almonds,
and pistachios
is nice)

1. In a medium saucepan, stir together the rice flour, sugar, caraway, anise seeds, cinnamon, and ginger until well combined. Add the water, and mix well. Set the pan and cook over medium heat, stirring constantly, until the mixture starts to thicken and reaches the consistency of pastry cream, about 30 minutes.

2. Pour into serving bowls, cover, and refrigerate for an hour.

3. Sprinkle each portion with 1 teaspoon of coconut and ½ tablespoon of chopped nuts right before serving.

SNAYNIEH
Sweetened Cracked Wheat with Anise

SERVES 8 / PREP TIME: 5 MINUTES / COOK TIME: 25 MINUTES

Snaynieh **comes from the word** *snan* **in Arabic, which means "teeth." It is served to guests to celebrate a baby's first tooth. It is very easy to make, requiring only a few ingredients. I love drizzling it with honey and topping it with sliced strawberries.**

4 cups water

2 tablespoons anise seeds

¾ cup cracked wheat

½ cup confectioners' sugar

1 teaspoon ground cinnamon

1 teaspoon orange blossom water

¼ cup mixed chopped nuts (a combination of pine nuts, blanched almonds, and pistachios is nice)

1. In a medium saucepan, bring the water to a boil.

2. Put the anise seeds into an infuser or a cheese-cloth secured with a string, and add to the boiling water.

3. Add the wheat, and reduce the heat to medium. Cook until tender and all of the liquid has been absorbed, about 25 minutes. It should have the consistency of a hearty soup. Remove from the heat. Remove the infuser.

4. Stir in the confectioners' sugar, cinnamon, and orange blossom water. Serve immediately, garnished with the nuts.

Tahini Sauce (Tahini), page 124

Chapter Nine

Basics
Asassiat

The following recipes for Lebanese "basics" will save you time in the kitchen and give you tools to bring authentic flavor to all of your dishes. For example, *Aliyyet Kezbara w Toum* (Sautéed Cilantro and Garlic), a flavorful combination of garlic and fresh cilantro, takes two minutes to make, but it is a crucial finishing touch for just about all Lebanese stews. It is what pulls all the flavors together and makes Lebanese stew stand out. Other recipes, like Kafta (Seasoned Ground Meat with Parsley) and Laban (Yogurt Stew), form the basis of numerous Lebanese dishes. Keep these basics in the refrigerator.

LAHMET KHAROUF LA TABEEKH
Cooked Lamb Cubes for Stew

SERVES 4 / PREP TIME: 5 MINUTES / COOK TIME: 40 MINUTES

I always like to have a stash of this meat in the refrigerator. It keeps for a few days, and it can be used to make a variety of stews and rice dishes.

½ cup vegetable oil

1 pound lamb stew
    meat, diced

3 yellow onions,
    finely chopped

2 cups water

5 cardamom pods

5 bay leaves

3 cinnamon sticks

1 tablespoon Lebanese
    7-Spice Blend
    (Baharat, page 121)

1 teaspoon sea salt

1 teaspoon freshly
    ground black pepper

1. In a large skillet, heat the oil over medium heat. Add the lamb and onions. Cook, stirring occasionally, until the meat has browned on all sides, about 10 minutes.

2. Stir in the water, cardamom, bay leaves, cinnamon, 7-spice blend, 1 teaspoon of salt, and the pepper. Cover, reduce the heat to low, and simmer until the lamb is tender, about 30 minutes. Strain through a fine-mesh strainer set over a bowl, reserving the liquid.

MAKE-AHEAD TIP: This dish stew will keep in an airtight container for up to a week in the refrigerator and up to 2 months in the freezer. Store the meat and broth separately.

KAFTA
Seasoned Ground Meat with Parsley

MAKES ABOUT 2 POUNDS / PREP TIME: 10 MINUTES

Kafta, a seasoned mixture of ground beef and lamb, can be used in many dishes. It can be grilled, baked, broiled, or fried. Stuff it into a pita, or serve it with rice or salad. I like using a blend of 75 percent beef top round and 25 percent leg of lamb or lamb shoulder. Lamb fat adds flavor and texture. If you like a bit of heat, add some diced jalapeño or other hot chile along with the parsley and onion.

1½ pounds beef top round, trimmed of excess fat

8 ounces boneless leg of lamb or lamb shoulder, trimmed of excess fat

1 cup fresh parsley leaves, including some stems

1 medium onion, diced

1 tablespoon Lebanese 7-Spice Blend (Baharat, page 121)

1 teaspoon sea salt

1. Using a meat grinder, grind the beef and lamb together to a coarse consistency.

2. Mix in the parsley, onion, 7-spice blend, and salt. Put through the grinder a second time.

INGREDIENT TIP: If you don't have a meat grinder, you can use already ground meat or have the butcher at your meat counter grind it for you. Finely chop the parsley and onion before adding them to the meat.

HASHWET LAHME
Seasoned Ground Meat with Pine Nuts

SERVES 4 / PREP TIME: 5 MINUTES / COOK TIME: 15 MINUTES

You can use all lamb or all beef for this dish, but a mixture of both is ideal. I like to use a half-and-half mixture of beef round and leg of lamb. This refrigerator staple makes it easy to whip up many dishes.

½ cup vegetable oil

1 large onion, chopped

1 pound ground meat
(beef, lamb, or both)

½ cup pine nuts,
toasted

1 teaspoon sea salt

1 teaspoon freshly
ground black pepper

1 teaspoon Lebanese
7-Spice Blend
(Baharat, page 121)

½ teaspoon ground
cinnamon

¼ teaspoon ground
cardamom

1. In a large skillet, heat the oil over medium heat. Add the onion, and cook, stirring frequently, until softened, about 5 minutes.

2. Add the ground meat, and cook, breaking up with a wooden spoon, until browned, about 10 minutes.

3. Add the pine nuts, salt, pepper, 7-spice blend, cinnamon, and cardamom. Stir gently to combine.

MAKE-AHEAD TIP: This dish will keep in an airtight container for up to a week in the refrigerator and up to 2 months in the freezer. Let cool before storing.

LABAN
Yogurt Stew

SERVES 4 / PREP TIME: 5 MINUTES / COOK TIME: 15 MINUTES

There are different ways of preparing yogurt stew. Some people like to add egg or egg whites to it. Some people use rice or flour instead of cornstarch as a thickener. I find the following recipe to be the easiest and least time consuming.

Laban is used as a base for many dishes, including Kibbe in Mint Yogurt Stew (Kibbe Labaniyeh, page 68) and Meat Dumplings in Yogurt Sauce (Shish Barak, page 69).

1 (32-ounce) container full-fat plain yogurt

½ cup cornstarch whisked with ½ cup water until smooth

1 teaspoon sea salt

1 teaspoon freshly ground white pepper

1 tablespoon extra-virgin olive oil

1 tablespoon minced garlic

1 teaspoon dried mint or 1 tablespoon chopped fresh cilantro

1. Put the yogurt in a medium saucepan over medium heat. Whisk in the cornstarch mixture. Cook, stirring, until starting to steam, about 5 minutes.

2. Stir in the salt and pepper. Reduce the heat to low, and simmer until thickened, about 3 minutes.

3. In a small sauté pan, heat the oil over medium-high heat. Add the garlic and mint. Cook, stirring, until browned, about 3 minutes. Stir into the yogurt, and cook, stirring, until thoroughly combined, about 2 minutes. Remove from the heat.

MAKE-AHEAD TIP: This stew will keep in an airtight container in the refrigerator for up to 3 days.

ZA'ATAR
Za'atar

MAKES ABOUT ¾ CUP / PREP TIME: 5 MINUTES

Za'atar is the king of Middle Eastern seasonings. It is so important to the cuisine, in fact, that I named my restaurant Au Za'atar. A sprinkling of za'atar adds amazing flavor to many dishes. Pita bread, extra-virgin olive oil with za'atar for dipping, and a dish of olives can make for a satisfying snack or even a simple meal. Every family has its own za'atar blend, varying the proportions of the herbs and spices. This version is my own.

1 tablespoon sesame seeds, toasted

¼ cup ground sumac

2 tablespoons dried thyme

2 tablespoons dried marjoram

2 tablespoons dried oregano

1 teaspoon sea salt

¼ teaspoon Aleppo chile flakes, or more to taste (optional)

1. Grind the sesame seeds in a food processor, or use a mortar and pestle. Transfer to a bowl.

2. Add the sumac, thyme, marjoram, oregano, salt, and chile flakes (if using). Mix well.

MAKE-AHEAD TIP: This seasoning will keep in an airtight container in a cool, dry place for up to 6 months.

BAHARAT
Lebanese 7-Spice Blend

MAKES 3 TABLESPOONS / PREP TIME: 5 MINUTES

This mixture of spices is used throughout Lebanon, though the exact proportions of the seven spices vary from region to region and family to family. This version uses allspice as the main flavor. You can adjust the proportions to your liking. You can use ground spices or, for more intense flavor, whole spices ground with a mortar and pestle or in a spice grinder. You'll use this seasoning in dishes such as Zucchini and Chickpea Stew (Mfarket Kousa, page 94), Seasoned Ground Meat with Pine Nuts (Hashwet Lahme, page 118), Seasoned Ground Meat with Parsley (Kafta, page 117), and Cooked Lamb Cubes for Stew (Lahmet Kharouf La Tabeekh, page 116).

1 tablespoon
    ground allspice

1 teaspoon ground
    cumin

1 teaspoon ground
    cinnamon

1 teaspoon ground
    ginger

1 teaspoon ground
    coriander

1 teaspoon ground
    cardamom

1 teaspoon freshly
    ground black pepper

In a small bowl, stir together the allspice, cumin, cinnamon, ginger, coriander, cardamom, and pepper.

MAKE-AHEAD TIP: This spice mix will keep in an airtight container in a cool, dry place for up to 6 months.

ALIYYET KEZBARA W TOUM
Sautéed Cilantro and Garlic

MAKES ABOUT 2 TABLESPOONS / PREP TIME: 5 MINUTES /
COOK TIME: 5 MINUTES

Aliyyet, sautéed garlic with fresh or dried herbs, is added to stews, especially yogurt-based stews, tomato-based stews like Okra Stew with Lamb (Bamiye Bi Lahme, page 75), and vegetable broth-based stews. Aliyyet should be dolloped onto and stirred into the stew just before serving. Try it with pita bread and pickles on the side.

2 tablespoons
  extra-virgin olive oil

2 tablespoons
  minced garlic

2 tablespoons chopped
  fresh cilantro

1. In a small sauté pan, heat the oil over medium-high heat.

2. Add the garlic and cilantro. Cook, stirring, until fragrant and the garlic has browned, about 2 minutes. Remove from the heat.

VARIATION
Aliyyet Na'ana w Toum / Sautéed Mint and Garlic:
Substitute 2 tablespoons of dried mint for the cilantro.

MAJUEN ELFILFIL
Roasted Pepper Paste

MAKES ABOUT 1 CUP / PREP TIME: 10 MINUTES / COOK TIME: 20 MINUTES

Pepper paste is one of those ingredients that can bring a special something to a dish. You can buy it premade in Middle Eastern stores, but it's not hard to make, and when you prepare it yourself, you can tailor it to your taste. For instance, you can leave out the chiles if you don't like heat.

3 red bell peppers

3 long red chiles, halved and seeded

Juice of ½ lemon

1 teaspoon sea salt

½ teaspoon freshly ground black pepper

1. Preheat the oven to 400°F.

2. Put the bell peppers and chiles on a baking sheet, and transfer to the oven. Roast, turning them once, until the skins blister and char, about 20 minutes. Remove from the oven. Let cool.

3. Once cool enough to handle, peel the bell peppers, and remove the stems, seeds, and membranes. Roughly chop, and put in a blender.

4. Use a sharp knife to scrape the flesh of the chiles away from the skins (this is easier than trying to peel them). Put them in the blender, and pulse to a fine purée.

5. With the motor running, add the lemon juice, salt, and pepper, and process until combined.

MAKE-AHEAD TIP: This paste will keep in an airtight container in the refrigerator for about a week.

TAHINI
Tahini Sauce

MAKES ABOUT 2 CUPS / PREP TIME: 5 MINUTES

Tahini sauce can be used as a dressing for sandwiches, especially red meat sandwiches made with shawarma, kafta kebab, or lamb kebab, and it is a must with Falafel (Falafel, page 23). It is also used in Baked Kafta in Tahini (Kafta Bi Tahini, page 65). When you add water to the tahini paste, it initially will look like a mess, and you may think you're not doing it right, but continue whisking until a silky, smooth sauce results.

1 tablespoon
    minced garlic

1 cup tahini paste,
    thoroughly stirred

1½ cups cold water

½ cup freshly squeezed
    lemon juice

1 tablespoon sea salt

1. In a large bowl, whisk together the garlic and tahini paste.

2. Whisking continuously, slowly add the cold water, then the lemon juice and salt. Continue whisking until the mixture is creamy and smooth.

MAKE-AHEAD TIP: This sauce will keep in an airtight container in the refrigerator for up to 3 days.

LABAN BI TAHINI
Yogurt-Tahini Sauce

MAKES ABOUT 4 CUPS / PREP TIME: 5 MINUTES

This sauce is a foundation for various *fatteh* dishes (dishes made with layers of pita chips). A good *Laban Bi Tahini* makes a fatteh stand out. It's a light, smooth sauce that combines tart yogurt with nutty tahini paste and garlic.

2 cups full-fat plain yogurt

½ cup tahini paste, thoroughly stirred

½ cup cold water

½ cup freshly squeezed lemon juice

¼ cup minced garlic

2 tablespoons sea salt

1. In a large bowl, whisk together the yogurt and tahini paste.

2. Whisking continuously, slowly add the cold water, then the lemon juice, garlic, and salt. Continue whisking until the mixture is creamy and smooth.

MAKE-AHEAD TIP: This dish will keep in an airtight container in the refrigerator for up to a week.

TOUM
Garlic Cream

MAKES ABOUT 4 CUPS / PREP TIME: 5 MINUTES

There are many recipes for toum, which can be thickened with cornstarch, boiled potatoes, or egg whites. This is my favorite way to make it: creamy, but still light and easy to digest. To get the right texture without breaking the emulsion, you need to add the oil slowly in a thin stream with your food processor running. This sauce is often spread on chicken sandwiches or served alongside grilled chicken, chicken kebabs, or marinated rotisserie chicken.

¼ cup garlic cloves, peeled

½ cup ice

2 large egg whites

¼ cup freshly squeezed lemon juice

1¼ teaspoons sea salt

3 cups vegetable oil

1. In a food processor, combine the garlic and the ice, and process.

2. Add the egg whites, and process until the mixture forms a paste, about 2 minutes.

3. Add the lemon juice and salt. Process until the mixture is smooth.

4. With the processor running, very slowly add the oil in a thin stream through the feed tube, processing until the mixture is creamy.

MAKE-AHEAD TIP: This sauce will keep in an airtight container in the refrigerator for up to 5 days.

A'ATER
Orange Blossom Syrup

MAKES ABOUT 2 CUPS / PREP TIME: 5 MINUTES, PLUS 1½ HOURS
TO CHILL / COOK TIME: 10 MINUTES

This fragrant syrup is essential to many Lebanese desserts and some fruit drinks. It is best to pour cold syrup on hot pastries and hot syrup on cold pastries; doing so helps the pastries absorb the flavor from the syrup.

1½ cups granulated sugar

¾ cup water

1 tablespoon freshly squeezed lemon juice

1 teaspoon orange blossom water, or more to taste

1. In a small saucepan, bring the sugar and water to a boil over medium heat, stirring until the sugar dissolves.

2. Reduce the heat to low, and simmer for 5 minutes.

3. Add the lemon juice, and simmer until thickened, about 5 minutes. Remove from the heat.

4. Stir in the orange blossom water. Add more to taste, one drop at a time, if needed, to achieve the concentration of flavor you prefer. Let cool for about 30 minutes, then refrigerate for 1 hour before using.

MAKE-AHEAD TIP: This syrup will keep in an airtight container in the refrigerator for up to a month.

Menus for Entertaining

Breaking the Fast at Ramadan

Ramadan is about family time and having meals together. For the month of Ramadan, people fast from sunrise to sunset. For the entire month, family members gather at the table at the end of each day to break their fasts. Ramadan is a month to which everyone looks forward. Restaurants serve huge buffets, pastry and dessert shops are fully loaded with sweets, families gather, and neighbors also visit with and cook for one another. In Lebanon we say, "If you eat alone, you die alone," and during Ramadan you won't find anyone eating alone, that is for sure.

After fasting all day, it is best to start with liquids such as water, yogurt drinks, and soup before having lighter dishes and then finally a main dish with rice and a salad. Ramadan feasts are everyone's favorite because of their variety. Fasting heightens the anticipation.

Red Lentil Soup (Shorbet Adas, page 93)

Fried Kibbe Stuffed with Spiced Beef and
Pine Nuts (Kibbe Krass, page 32)

Yogurt-Cucumber Salad
(Laban Bi Keyar, page 41)

Chopped Seasonal Vegetable and Bread
Salad (Fattoush, page 39)

Baked Kafta Casserole (Kafta Bil-Saniyeh, page 64)

Rice Pilaf (Rezz Mfalfal, page 86)

Sweet Fritters (Aiwmat, page 107)

Christmas Dinner

Christmas is very festive in Lebanon, and families gather together to celebrate, so small plates are ideal. On holidays, you'll usually find different generations of women preparing the feast while the rest of the family and friends chat and visit in anticipation of the meal to come.

Hummus (Hummus, page 18)

———

Baba Ghanoush
(Mtabal Batengane, page 20)

———

Yogurt Cheese Dip
(Labne, page 10)

———

Fried Cauliflower
(Arnabeet Mekli, page 25)

———

Spinach Pies
(Fatayer Sbanek, page 30)

———

Fried Kibbe Stuffed with Spiced Beef
and Pine Nuts
(Kibbe Krass, page 32)

———

Rice Pilaf
(Rezz Mfalfal, page 86)

———

Lamb and Yogurt Stew with
Mint and Garlic
(Laban Immo, page 68)

———

Ma'amoul (Ma'amoul, page 102)
or Colored Sweet Fritters
(Mshabbak, page 109)

———

Sit-Down Dinner

A sit-down meal will be served in courses, starting with cold mezze and salads. The next course will feature hot mezze, and it will be followed by some combination of fish, chicken, or meat dishes and, finally, dessert. When doing your planning, take timing and proximity into consideration: If the table you will be dining at is in or near the kitchen, consider preparing dishes that don't require your entire attention, so that you can cook for, welcome, and serve your guests without feeling overwhelmed. If you will be eating far from your kitchen, even more preparation will be required.

Here are some phrases that will put you in good stead, as a guest and as a host, with Lebanese family and friends: *Ahla w sahla* means "you are welcome in my home," *daymeh* means "may your table be always blessed," and *a'a albek habibi* means "for your health, my dear."

Hummus
(Hummus, page 18)

———

Baba Ghanoush
(Mtabal Batengane,
page 20)

———

Fried Kibbe Stuffed with
Spiced Beef and Pine Nuts
(Kibbe Krass, page 32)

———

Chopped Parsley, Tomato,
and Bulgur Salad
(Tabouli, page 38)

———

Parsley-Tahini Salad
(Saltet Taratour, page 44)

Chopped Seasonal
Vegetable and Bread Salad
(Fattoush, page 39)

———

Tomato and Red
Onion Salad
(Saltet el-Banadoura,
page 40)

———

Fried Smelts
(Samak Bizri-Mekli,
page 58)

———

Fish with Lemon and
Pine Nut Sauce
(Samak Ma'at-
Taratour, page 56)

———

Lebanese Bread Pudding
(Aysh El Saraya, page 111)

Buffet for Friends and Family

For a buffet, we'll serve impressive-looking dishes, such as stuffed lamb shoulder, leg of lamb, lamb ribs, or fish. Make it easy on yourself by doing as much prep as you can. You'll see my suggestions throughout the following list.

Hummus (Hummus, page 18)
(make the day before, mixing in the garlic
and lemon juice right before serving)

———————

Baba Ghanoush
(Mtabal Batengane, page 20)
(make the day before, mixing in the garlic
and lemon juice right before serving)

———————

Spinach Pies
(Fatayer Sbanek, page 30)
(make the day before, and reheat)

———————

Vegetarian Stuffed Grape Leaves
(Warra' Einab Bil Zeit, page 27)
(make 2 to 3 days before)

———————

Fried Kibbe Stuffed with Spiced Beef
and Pine Nuts
(Kibbe Krass, page 32)
(make the day before, and reheat)

———————

Chopped Parsley, Tomato,
and Bulgur Salad (Tabouli, page 38)
(prepare the day before; mix with the
dressing right before serving)

———————

Chopped Seasonal Vegetable and Bread Salad
(Fattoush, page 39)
(prepare the day before; mix with the
dressing right before serving)

————————

Cabbage Salad
(Saltet Malfouf, page 42)

————————

Yogurt-Cucumber Salad
(Laban Bi Keyar, page 41)

————————

Yogurt-Braised Lamb Ribs
(Dala'a Mehshi, page 73)

————————

Baked Garlic Chicken with
Potatoes (Djej w Batata
Bil-Saniyeh, page 82)

————————

Grilled Sea Bass
(Samak Meshwi, page 53)

————————

Rice and Vermicelli Pilaf
(Rezz Bil Sh'ariyeh, page 87)

————————

Potatoes with Cilantro and Cumin
(Batata w Kezbara, page 90)

————————

Baklava (Baklawa, page 104)
(make 2 or 3 days ahead)

————————

Glossary of Arabic Terms

ahla w sahla: welcome

banadoura: tomato

bassal: onion

batata: potato

batengane: eggplant

beid: eggs

bharat: spices

kabees: pickles

kousa: zucchini

laban: yogurt

maslooʾa: boiled

mekli: fried

meshwi al fahim: grilled on charcoal

meshwi bil forn: grilled in the oven

mouneh: in short, "pantry," but also refers to preserving perishable foods to extend their shelf life

mshakal: assorted

rezz: rice

sahtain: bon appétit

saltet: salad

shoaʾaf: cubes

shoukran: thank you

tabeekh: home-cooked food

tawla: table

toum: garlic

yakne: stew

zeit: oil

Resources

www.ziyad.com

www.kalustyans.com

www.hashems.com

www.sahadis.com

www.usacortas.com

www.baroodyimports.com

www.alwadi-alakhdar.com

Measurement Conversions

OVEN TEMPERATURES

Fahrenheit	Celsius (approximate)
250°F	120°C
300°F	150°C
325°F	165°C
350°F	180°C
375°F	190°C
400°F	200°C
425°F	220°C
450°F	230°C

WEIGHT EQUIVALENTS

US Standard	Metric (approximate)
½ ounce	15 g
1 ounce	30 g
2 ounces	60 g
4 ounces	115 g
8 ounces	225 g
12 ounces	340 g
16 ounces or 1 pound	455 g

VOLUME EQUIVALENTS (LIQUID)

US Standard	US Standard (ounces)	Metric (approximate)
2 tablespoons	1 fl. oz.	30 mL
¼ cup	2 fl. oz.	60 mL
½ cup	4 fl. oz.	120 mL
1 cup	8 fl. oz.	240 mL
1½ cups	12 fl. oz.	355 mL
2 cups or 1 pint	16 fl. oz.	475 mL
4 cups or 1 quart	32 fl. oz.	1 L
1 gallon	128 fl. oz.	4 L

VOLUME EQUIVALENTS (DRY)

US Standard	Metric (approximate)
⅛ teaspoon	0.5 mL
¼ teaspoon	1 mL
½ teaspoon	2 mL
¾ teaspoon	4 mL
1 teaspoon	5 mL
1 tablespoon	15 mL
¼ cup	59 mL
⅓ cup	79 mL
½ cup	118 mL
⅔ cup	156 mL
¾ cup	177 mL
1 cup	235 mL
2 cups or 1 pint	475 mL
3 cups	700 mL
4 cups or 1 quart	1 L

Index

About the Author

Tarik Fallous is a chef and restaurateur. He learned how to cook traditional Lebanese food from his mother before moving to the United States from Lebanon at the age of 19. He is executive chef/owner at Au Za'atar Restaurant, in New York City's East Village neighborhood. At his restaurant, he highlights the best of Lebanese and Middle Eastern cuisine, with a focus on fresh, seasonal ingredients and home-style dishes.

CPSIA information can be obtained
at www.ICGtesting.com
Printed in the USA
JSHW020313191221
21336JS00005B/5